Sparano+Mooney Architecture

A Way of Working

SPARANO + MOONEY

A R C H I T E C T U R E:

A WAY OF WORKING

HATJE
CANTZ

Contents

This book is dedicated to our parents, who have made this work possible, and to our daughters, Claire Elizabeth and Audrey Therese, who inspire us every day.

John Sparano + Anne Mooney

Preface

For over two decades, Sparano + Mooney Architecture has been quietly mapping our intentions through architecture, making ideas visible in the world as inhabitable space. In 1997, from a modest rental in Venice, California, we founded our practice. From the start, we have been committed to doing whatever it takes to produce well-considered architecture for an audience who cares deeply about design.

Architecture possesses the ability to communicate through its silent presence. Its space, form, scale, proportion, material, and detail express the unique set of circumstances from which a design emerges. These circumstances include the physical, environmental, and cultural context of architecture, and of course, its place in time. As architects, we have to insist that this world can be other than it currently is. Our work represents an attempt to express the possibilities that lie within our medium, architecture. It is here that we are able to contribute to the world by offering experiences crafted of space, light, and shadow.

We also seek a deep understanding of context in our work. Through our design process, we bring into focus the essential nature of place. While keeping in mind the responsibility of designing places in which people dwell, we recognize architecture is part of a larger context where the work responds and contributes. A particular time and its physical and cultural environment set the framework for generating ideas. As a core concept emerges, whether explicitly stated or not, it establishes the foundation upon which architecture is built. The program, the site, the cultural or environmental context, and the material expression are each woven together through this central organizing idea.

The architecture we bring forth is not separate from the process by which it has been produced—the two are intertwined. Our path is not linear but one of continual testing until the essential nature of a work and its latent potential are revealed. This often messy process of discovery takes place not only in the workday in our studio but also in exploring a site, spending time in conversation together or alone, confronting the terror of a blank sheet in the sketchbook.

Our process attempts to slow the technical prowess of contemporary architectural production tools in a continual attempt to return to what is essential. This invariably involves the hand—in our sketching, drawing, modeling, making, and writing the architecture. We begin with a process of writing, gathering, filtering, and, especially, spending those early days with eyes wide open. It is rarely an easy, graceful process to excruciatingly extract the right idea at precisely the right moment.

We have always sought a connection between ourselves and our environment. These relationships are strongest when they are forged at the most elemental levels. Light, gravity, and form have all played major roles in creating bonds between a culture and its architecture precisely because of their fundamental roles in shaping an experience of space. Without illumination, we struggle to fully experience architecture, gravity is structure's raison d'être, and form embodies meaning.

The inhabitant of architecture is always in motion. In approaching, passing by, and going through architecture, one comes to understand space dynamically. This is as fundamental to our understanding of the physical world as our capacity to collect memories over a lifetime. In uncovering the nascent within a project and exploring what should be revealed through our design process lie the poetics and potential of our practice. In the end, we seek to provide the world with enduring architectural experiences.

—Anne Mooney, Principal and Cofounder

INTRODUCTION

Never in history have architects enjoyed greater freedom to realize their wildest dreams. Computer software has liberated designers, engineers, and contractors to create buildings of dazzling complexity that seem to defy the laws of physics. Too often, form loses touch with function and becomes an end in itself—a lure to fundraisers or prospective occupants. That is why many of the best architects continue to play variations, bold or subtle, on a few basic forms. It is they who enhance our cities and landscapes, tailoring buildings to the site and the needs of their users. For more than twenty years, the husband-wife partnership of John Sparano and Anne Mooney has been doing just that: crafting houses, community centers, museums, and ambitious projects with a passion for materiality, nature, and the spirit of place.

The firm has no signature—every project is freshly thought-out—but there is a DNA that threads through the work, creating a sense of continuity. Many of its buildings are in remote locations, so materials must be low-maintenance and age well. Board-formed concrete, wood, and rusting steel are favorites for their rich tones and textures, and their organic relationship to the land. Budgets are often tight, and the architects have turned frugality to their advantage, finding beauty in unadorned simplicity. They welcome the challenge of building in the wild, where a rectangle or square defines a facade and frames the landscape or distant city lights. The urban buildings are responsive to context and are often layered to give them a sense of depth. Above all, their architecture is sensory and experiential—a hard thing to capture on the printed page.

In Southern California, the architects open up their living spaces almost year-round; in mountain country, they employ visual devices to draw the outside in. Though the state of Utah has yet to adopt strict environmental standards, the architects encourage their clients to invest in the latest technologies, and Park City (like Los Angeles) requires that new public buildings be zero-energy. Every house has radiant heating, and passive strategies take care of cooling on all but a few summer days. Clients appreciate the firm's heating and cooling expertise, which includes the use of photovoltaic panels charging Tesla batteries.

Sparano and Mooney launched their architectural practice in Los Angeles in 1997 and expanded to Salt Lake City in 2004. Though they still maintain a productive office in LA, Utah has become a principal field of activity, where they work with a team of collaborators. Having one foot in the wilderness and one in the metropolis enriches their work. Complementary talents and shared values make Sparano + Mooney Architecture an unusually productive studio, one that intends to stay small but tackles larger projects as those opportunities arise. Currently, the studio is collaborating with Elemental, the Chilean firm headed by Pritzker laureate Alejandro Aravena, on the design of the headquarters for the Sundance Institute and its renowned film festival in nearby Park City.

As a youth, Sparano had a passion for making things and quickly realized he wanted to become an architect. At age twelve, he even formed a club with two school friends and sent away for house plans to collect and copy. A three-month tour of Europe inspired him to enroll in the Architectural Association in London, and when he moved to Los Angeles in 1990, he took a job with a large office, providing him with solid grounding in project management as well as design.

Mooney came to architecture by chance, having previously intended to follow her father's lead and become a pilot. She went to graduate school at Columbia, then switched to the Southern California Institute of Architecture, where one of her professors was the maverick architect Eric Owen Moss, with whom she interned.

For her, inspiration comes from the modernist pioneers Rudolph Schindler and Richard Neutra, the textile block houses of Frank Lloyd Wright, the early exploratory work of Frank Gehry, the restraint and refinement of Peter Zumthor, and the Dominus Winery of Herzog & de Meuron, with its porous walls of rock-filled gabions. Sparano names Steven Holl—an architect they both admire—as a model for his early work and his practice of starting every job with a concept, expressed by Holl in watercolors.

Sparano and Mooney follow a similar course, looking for a foundational idea that derives from a client, site, program, object, or text. They create small sculptures—heuristic devices to serve as a point of departure—and these are explored at length in Hikmet Sidney Loe's essay "Conceptual Constructs: Sparano + Mooney's Investigative Art of Architecture" (page 69). The concepts expressed in these sculptures are developed through sketches, multimedia studies, and collaborative discussions. Everyone in the office, from interns to founding partners, is invited to contribute ideas to flesh out the core concept. Then comes a guiding text and a physical model to engage the client in the creative process.

The best buildings emerge from a dialogue between architect and client, and this practice has built a relationship of trust with clients who have the inclination to try something different. In doing so, they challenge the great paradox of the West: a territory settled by pioneers fleeing the constraints of the Old World and the rigid hierarchies of eastern cities increasingly conservative in their tastes. Today, there's an influx of migrants from West and East Coast metropolises. People move to Utah, Montana, and Wyoming in search of the wilderness as well as a quieter, more affordable lifestyle. National parks preserve the illusion of an uncorrupted Eden, but too often culture trumps nature. Pale copies of historic styles predominate in sprawling suburbs, here as elsewhere.

Sparano and Mooney discovered a region that is still not fully formed, offering unlimited scope for creativity and an opportunity to make a statement. The built context is less important than the topography, allowing them to focus on environmental concerns and strengthening a sense of community. Like the Land artists who fled the conventions and constraints of East Coast galleries and museums to find a new canvas in the plains and deserts of the West, these architects are inspired by the heroic scale of the landscapes. Rocks and mountains provide inspiration that is distilled into tiny maquettes before emerging as buildings that are uniquely expressive of their sites. As Mooney observes, "A lot of our projects exist on the edges," on virgin ground or in modest neighborhoods.

Sparano + Mooney's buildings are reductive and uncompromisingly modern, efficient, and economical. They incorporate lessons from the siting of Native-American settlements, from log cabins and barns, and even from abandoned mining structures. They seek to reinterpret the vernacular, studying what can be learned from the humblest of dwellings in withstanding the extremes of heat and cold, storms and snow loads. Their architecture is a foil to nature and city streets, restrained in form and scaled to its surroundings, with an appropriate palette of materials and color.

The Urban Treehouse, located in a century-old neighborhood of Salt Lake City, demonstrates the architects' skill in standing out while fitting in, as well as the tolerance of local residents for a radical departure from traditional forms. The house is an extrusion of black wood, as minimal as a Donald Judd box, occupying a long, narrow site on a picture-pretty street of shingled cottages shaded by mature trees. The facade is set back to create a dark, cave-like portico, which serves as a protected gathering place, mediating between the street and the lofty great room beyond. A bridge spans a pool court, linking the living room to sleeping areas in the back. Despite its stark originality, neighbors have welcomed this new kid on the block, not least because it replaces a crack house. In sophisticated cities along the East and West Coasts of the United States, innovation is often discouraged, even contested, by residents anxious to preserve the status quo. Neighborhood associations and design review boards can impose conformity and banality on new developments. In Utah, despite the conservative preferences, almost anything is allowed—good and bad.

There's another striking juxtaposition in the mountainous terrain to the east of the city. A sprawling mega-mansion dominates the skyline as you ascend the slope, a jarring intrusion on the soft folds of the land. Around the next bend in the road is the Wabi-Sabi house designed by Sparano + Mooney, a floating composition as restrained as the Japanese aesthetic from which it takes its cues. Living and sleeping areas are contained in two cantilevered bars of space that radiate out from the entry and frame mountain views. Inspiration came from Nancy Holt's *Sun Tunnels* (1973–76), an important example of Land Art located in Utah's Great Basin Desert. From below, the glazing at the end of each bar reads as a mirror held up to nature. The sharp-edged geometry complements the organic forms of the landscape, each heightening awareness of the other. It's an example of what Neutra called "the machine in the garden."

A third example of the architects' gift for place-making is Saint Joseph the Worker Catholic Church. Located in a working-class district of Salt Lake City, it replaces a simple construction built by miners in 1964 following a prolonged strike. Thus, it plays a dual role: as a spiritual enclave and as a memorial to the struggles of a community. Boldly textured concrete is employed for the oval church and the pyramidal day chapel, both top-lit from copper-clad lanterns. The concrete expresses the hand of the craftsperson and emphasizes the permanence of the sacred spaces, in contrast to the wood-clad parish offices, an L-plan block that shields the courtyard from a busy roadway. A low concrete wall surrounds the courtyard, and there's a strong sense of axiality leading in from the parking lot. This axis then turns ninety degrees to lead you through a pivoting door and into the church. Curved wood pews radiate from the sanctuary like ripples on a pond and are raked to improve the sight lines. In contrast to the rigor of the church interior, the day chapel is lined with finely crafted Douglas fir.

These three projects, and seven others described in this monograph, exemplify the versatility of Sparano and Mooney's practice. Each has a distinct identity, responding to site and program, but there's a family resemblance in the simplicity of the forms and the emphasis on materiality. They are rooted, earthy, and tactile; some rough, some refined, but always with a sense of rightness that makes them seem inevitable. Each is conceived as a sanctuary, whether secular or spiritual, a serene oasis to nurture the senses and inspire awareness of nature, history, or the arts. They are designed from the inside out. Complex computer-generated shapes may excite attention and then lose their allure. The buildings of Sparano + Mooney Architecture will endure.

Nora Eccles Harrison Museum of Art

The Nora Eccles Harrison Museum of Art (NEHMA) is an academic art museum located on Utah State University's campus in the northern part of Utah. The museum is known for its outstanding collection of modern and contemporary art, and serves a broad regional audience with its exhibitions, programs, and events. The scope of this project encompassed the renovation and a major addition to NEHMA,[i] including the design of a new three-story, eight-thousand-square-foot addition with archival space housing a permanent collection consisting of over five thousand artworks by almost two thousand artists. Significant works in the collection include ceramics, paintings, drawings, and sculpture.

The project's primary goals were to upgrade the museum to an institution that could protect and accommodate world-class works of art and traveling exhibitions, and increase visibility and public access to the museum and its collections. The design provides patrons a new museum experience and creates a strong campus presence, embedding this key cultural asset for students, faculty, staff, and the public as they circulate through the campus. The former museum entrance was difficult to find, prompting the architects to reconsider the entry sequence and create an open facade that allows pedestrian circulation through an accessible, three-dimensional threshold experience. This newly created campus connection fosters interaction with both the architecture and the collection, and offers an enhanced pedestrian encounter activating this area of campus.

The design presents a new, quietly restrained form for the museum. The architecture does not compete with the adjacent signature building, a 2006 Sasaki-designed performing arts center facing the museum to the west.[ii] Rather, NEHMA creates a new public plaza that connects the two buildings in an almost neutral response to an already visually complex context. Adjacent to this corridor with diverse building forms, programs, scales, and materials, the architects opted for an architecture of quiet refinement in dialogue, not in competition, with what exists. The design response to this environment is a simple vertical screen of zinc cladding, referencing the materiality of the performing arts building but not the expressive form. The line between indoor and outdoor is blurred through this perforated zinc screen, and the programs and spaces flow out of the building into adjacent landscaped patios on the campus.

The porosity of the facade invites glimpses into the museum by passersby, and at night, the activity and exhibitions housed within glow through the building skin. By separating this screen from the architectural envelope at the plaza level, the campus traffic flows directly into and through the museum. The facade creates a space of transition and entry along its perforated veil, softly defining a new edge for the campus arts node. This welcoming sequence invites students of all disciplines to consider the role of art and creative endeavor in their lives and their education within the American tradition of the land-grant college.[iii] By opening up views of the collection to the campus through the building facade, the museum's charge of revealing new knowledge to visitors is now being realized during daily activity and, quietly, at night.

i

The original building was designed by Edward Larrabee Barnes, an influential American architect based in New York with a prolific body of work throughout the United States. Barnes was commissioned to design part of Caine College of the Arts at USU, including NEHMA, completing the project in 1982. This complex was his only work in Utah.

ii

Sasaki Associates is an architecture, design, and planning office headquartered in Watertown, Massachusetts. In 2006, the office completed the design of the Manon Caine Russell Kathryn Caine Wanlass Performance Hall, with a formally complex facade, located on the western edge of the fine arts complex at USU.

iii

Land-grant universities are designated institutions of higher learning formed to receive benefits of the Morrill Acts of 1862, 1890, and 1994, involving the exchange of federal land for colleges providing broad education in programs, including agriculture. This program led to the establishment of many universities, including Native and historically Black institutions, and opened the door for public higher education in the United States.

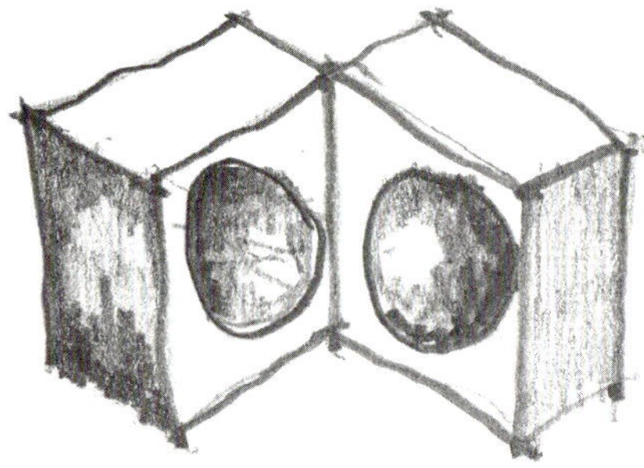

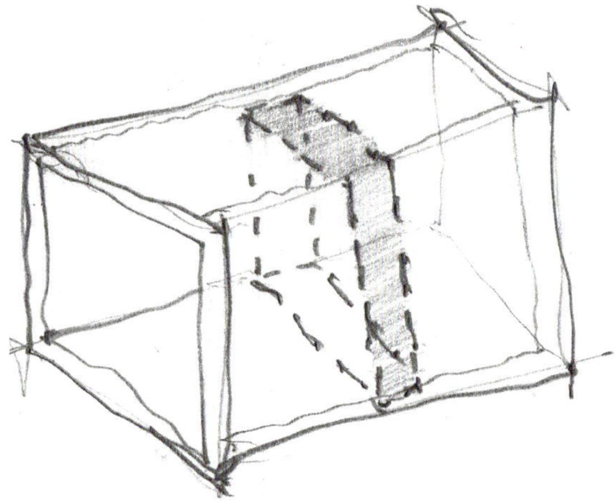

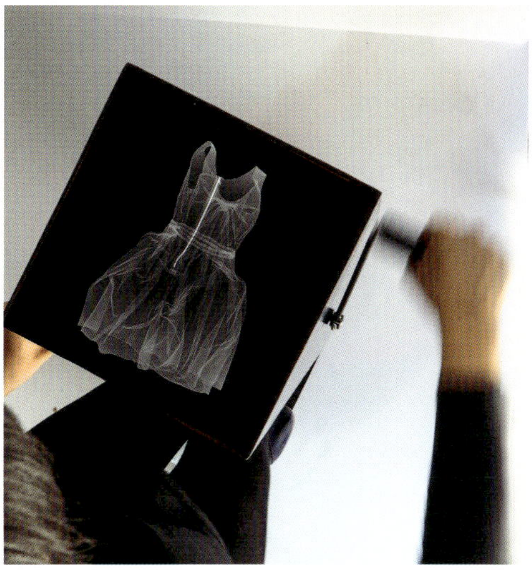

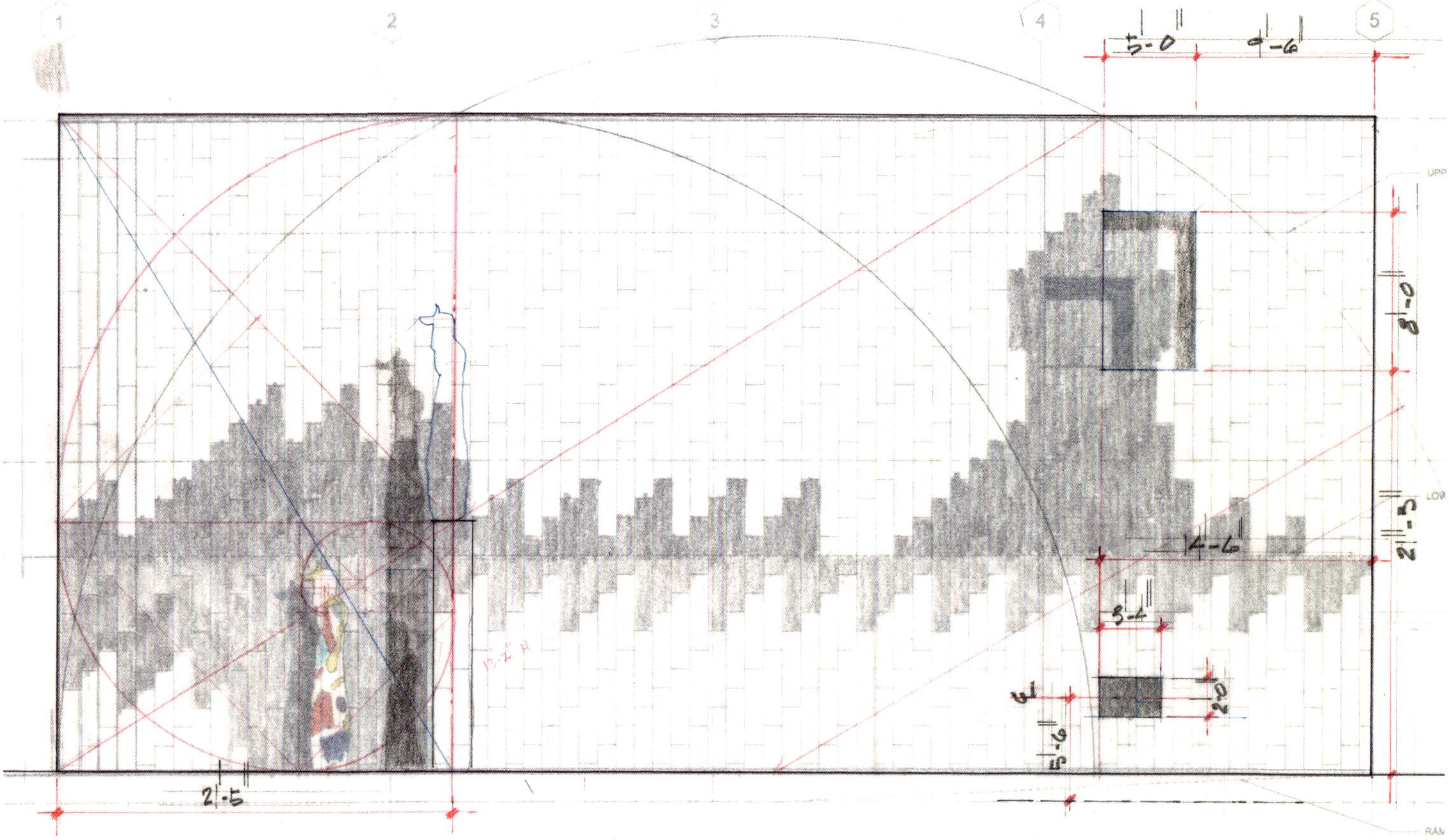
1
2
3
4
5
5-0
4-6
8-0
14-6
3-4
2-0
5-6
21-3
2-5

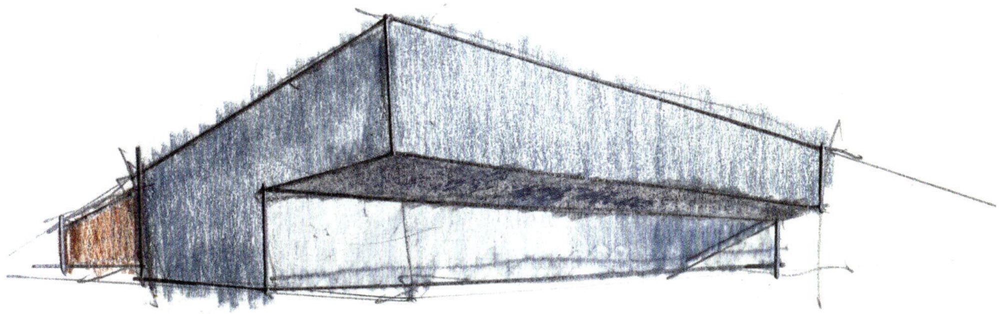

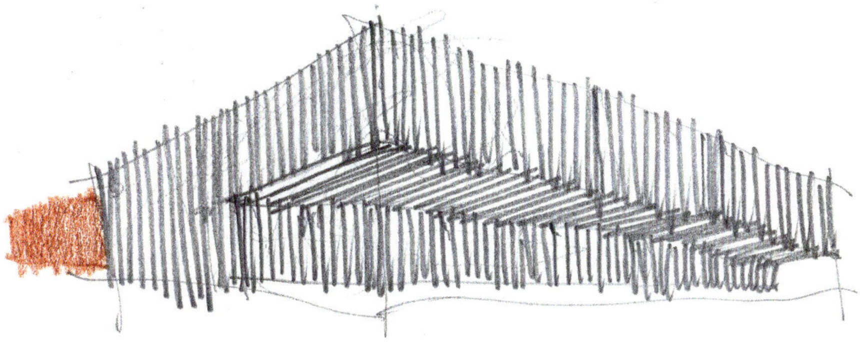

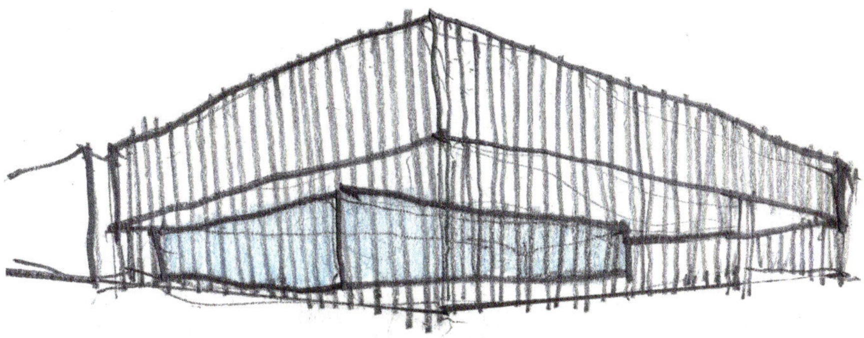

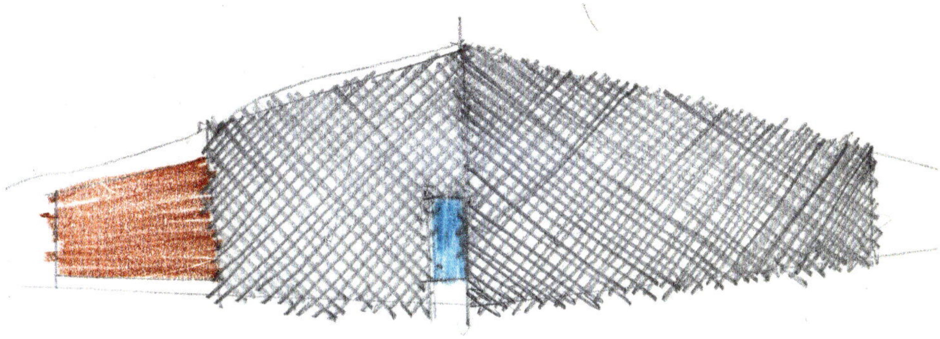

NORA ECCLES HARRISON MUSEUM OF ART
PERFORMANCE HALL

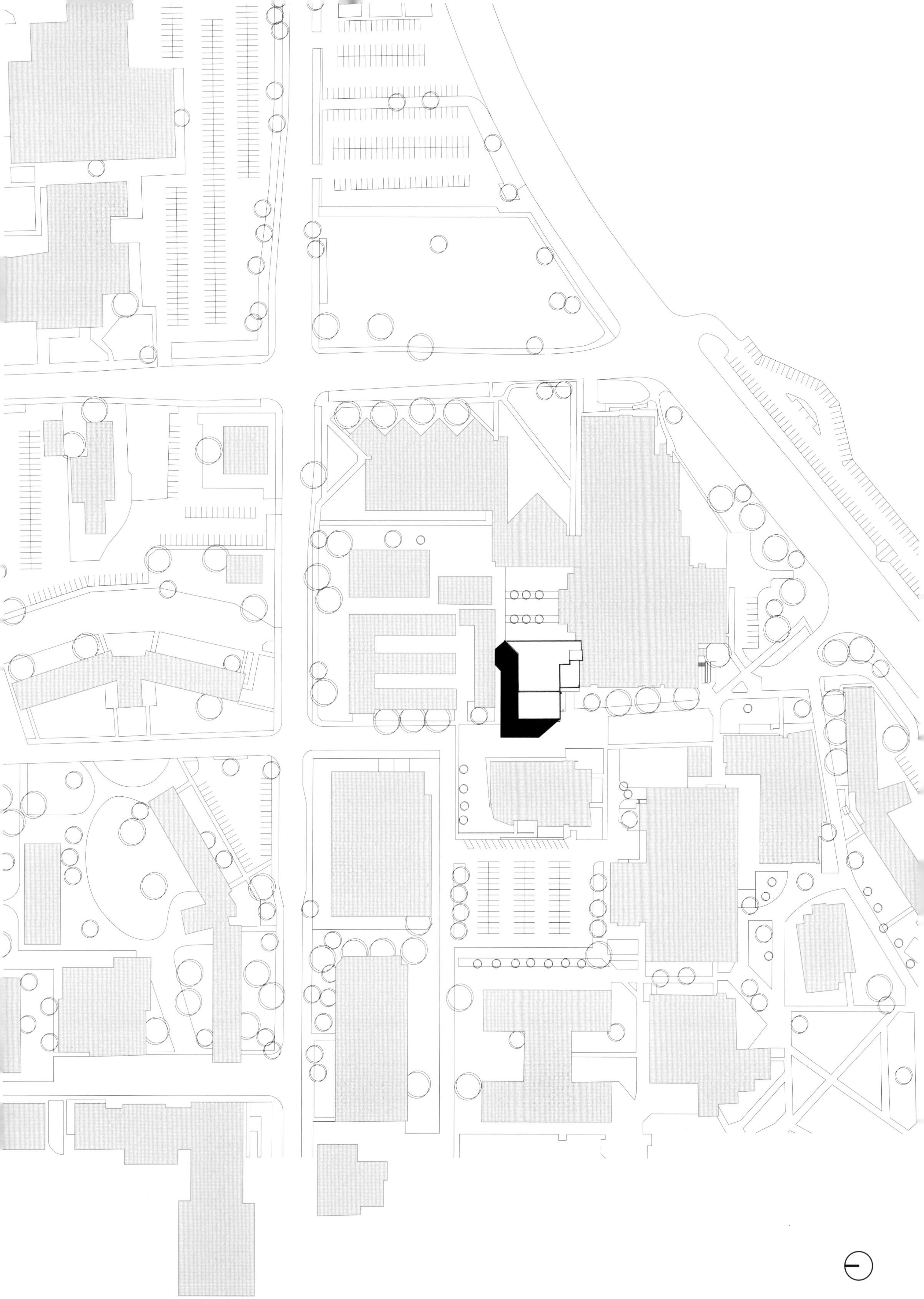

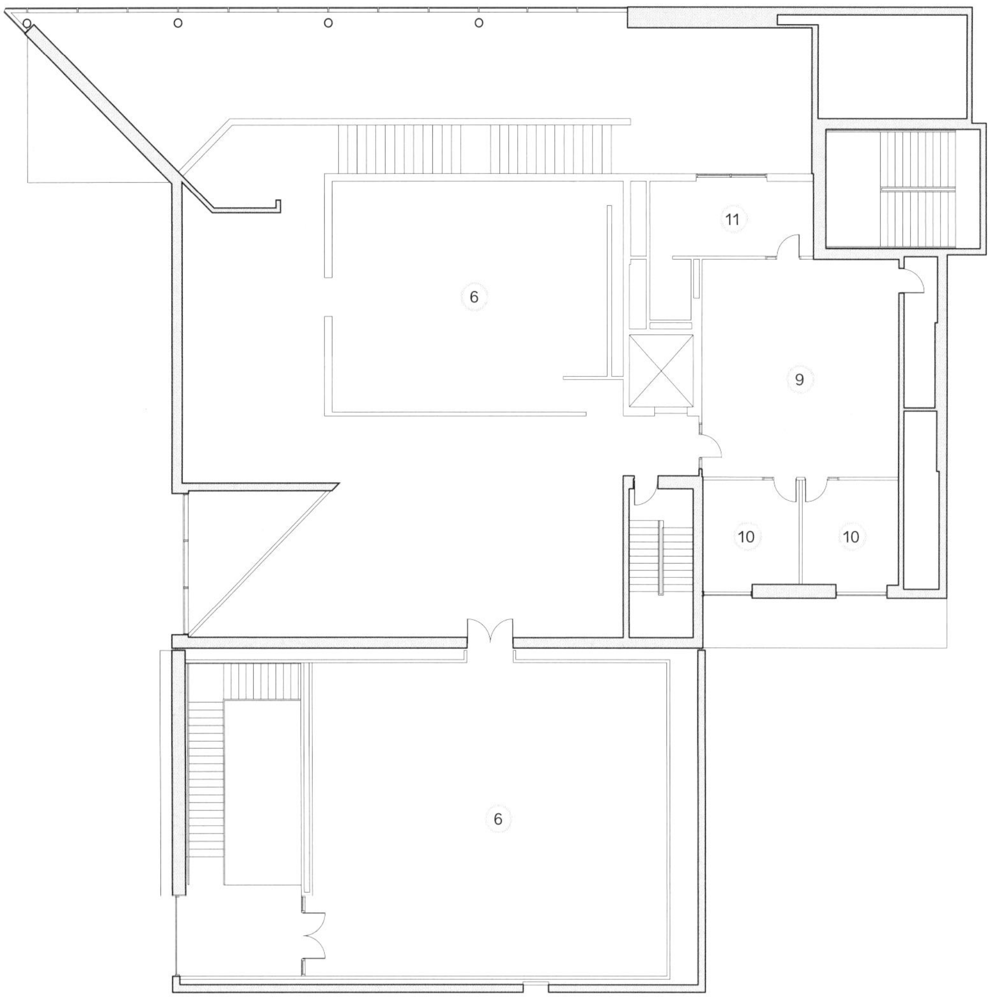

Upper Level

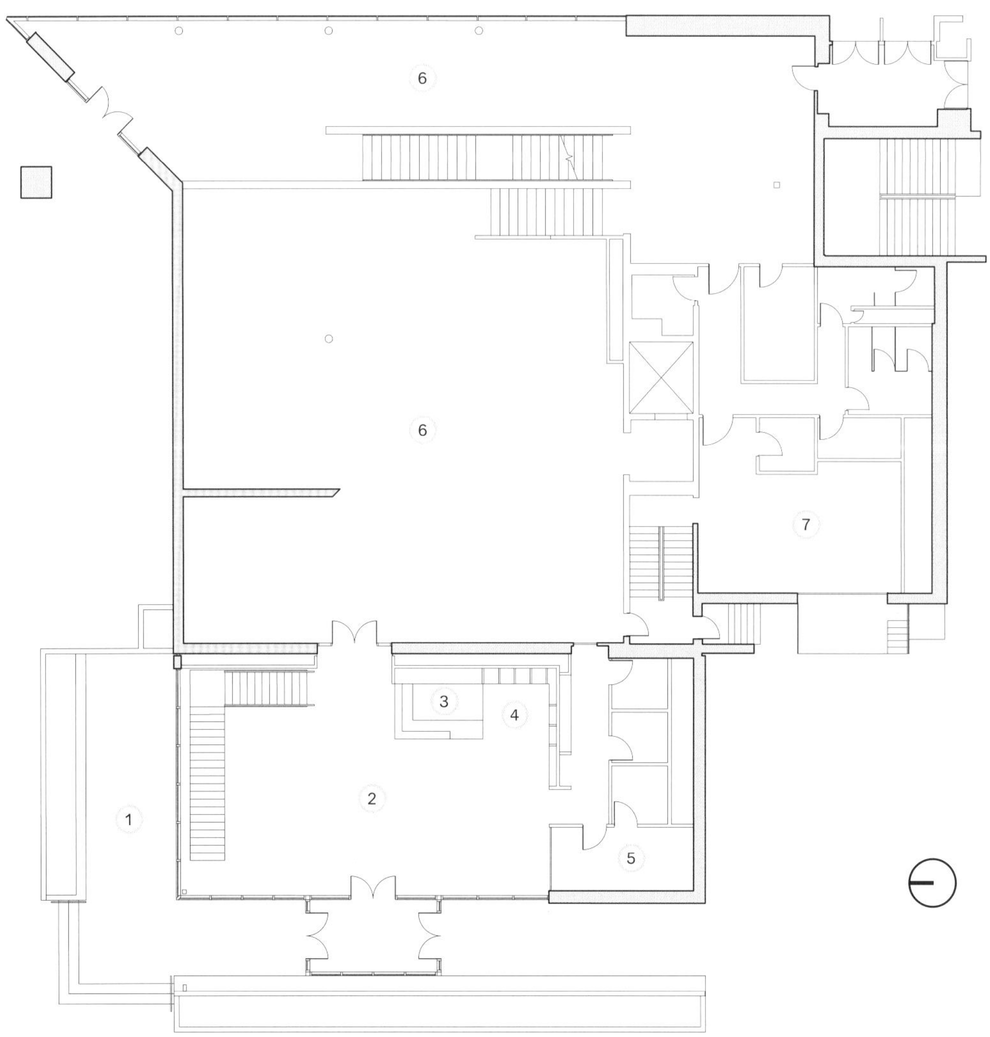

Main Level

1 Courtyard
2 Lobby
3 Info
4 Museum Store
5 Café
6 Gallery
7 Loading Dock
8 Art Storage (Lower Level)
9 Open Work Area
10 Office
11 Conference Room

NORA ECCLES HARRISON MUSEUM OF ART

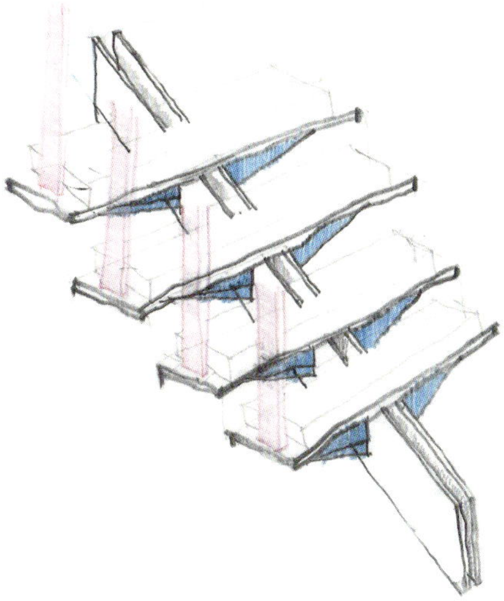

NORA ECCLES HARRISON MUSEUM OF ART

Image Captions

1 West facade (detail); © Jeremy Bittermann
2 Concept sketches; John Sparano
3 Final heuristic device
4 Study models
5 Study models
6 Elevation study; John Sparano
7 Massing study sketches; John Sparano
8 Fenestration studies
9 North and West facades; © Jeremy Bittermann
10 West facade, daytime view; © Jeremy Bittermann
11 West facade, evening view; © Jeremy Bittermann
12 Final model
Museum cross-section
13 Site plan
14 Upper-level floor plan
Main-level floor plan
15 Evening view; © Jeremy Bittermann
16 Museum staircase, view from second floor; © Jeremy Bittermann
17 Concept sketch for stair design; John Sparano
Museum staircase; © Jeremy Bittermann
18 Museum entry; © Jeremy Bittermann

Completed	2018
Size	8,000 SF (743 m^2)
Location	Logan, Utah
Client	Utah State University Katie Lee-Koven, Executive Director of NEHMA
Team	John Sparano Anne Mooney Seth Striefel Nate King Philip Dimick Jun Li Mark James (model)
Collaborators	Walt Crimm Associates (museum consultants) Calder Richards Consulting Engineers (structural engineering) Van Boerum and Frank Associates (mechanical engineering) Spectrum Engineers (electrical engineering) Cache Landmark (landscape architecture)
General Contractor	Gramoll Construction

Aurora Villa

The Aurora Villa is a boutique hotel located outside of Fairbanks, Alaska, on a remote wooded site. Known internationally as one of the ideal locations in the world to view the aurora borealis, it is where guests hope to catch a rare glimpse of the earth's natural light display.[i] Ephemeral and enchanting, the northern lights have fascinated and haunted people with their spectral presence for millennia. Over the past decade, there has been a surge in international tourism to remote and icy locales in Alaska, where the aurora borealis can best be viewed and photographed.

The project was designed following best practices for maintaining and supporting access to dark skies. These design principles minimize light emissions from the small resort. No artificial lighting is directed upward, and illumination within the site is minimized and subdued. By carefully considering the lighting strategy, the night sky and the area's wildlife habitats are protected, and unobstructed stargazing is possible.

The lodge is oriented to provide clear viewing of the northern lights. It offers private guest suites and public gathering spaces for community lounging in anticipation of the lights, with opportunities to socialize and share a meal in the communal dining hall. The architecture's large glazed openings are oriented toward floor-to-ceiling unobstructed views from key spaces in the lodge.

The architecture creates an environment designed to be experienced at night. During the day, guests are outside—dogsledding, viewing wildlife, or visiting the city of Fairbanks. At night, they return to the villa in anticipation of capturing glimpses of the aurora borealis. The lodge offers this unique nighttime experience in darkened rooms with carefully positioned LED lighting. This low-voltage lighting provides optimal conditions for photographers capturing images of the night sky.[ii]

The villa's exterior, comprised of cedarwood cladding and soffits, fits contextually within the landscape. Extreme climate conditions and a short construction season were prime considerations in developing the design, which incorporates a highly insulated building envelope and high-performance, low-energy-use systems.[iii]

Outdoor spaces include decks for photography, a spa, and an entry court. Landscape concepts were focused on reducing the impact of the architecture on the site with minimal removal of trees and restoring the native context. Due to the site's undulating topography and the positioning of the building on top of a slope, few trees were removed, and the architects were able to design spaces with optimal access to the panoramic views. Interior spaces feature these views of the landscape and sky as the primary visual "artwork."

The guest roster is composed primarily of international tourists in search of adventure in the heart of the American wilderness. The design reflects this spirit with its pure architectural forms and sophisticated interior design.

i

The aurora borealis, also referred to as the northern or polar lights, is a natural, often dramatic light display visible in the night sky in high-latitude regions of the planet. Alaska has emerged as a global leader in astro tourism, offering visitors access to stargazing and dark skies, both of which are increasingly endangered in many parts of the world. Optimal viewing of the aurora borealis is between September and April.

ii

The lighting incorporates a red LED system controlled centrally to preserve guests' views of the night sky. The red color limits eye dilation to allow for better night vision in the low-voltage LED system designed for energy conservation. Exterior lighting is directed downward to protect the night sky and minimize disruption to wildlife migration and mating patterns.

iii

Extreme weather conditions prompted the specification of a triple-glazed storefront system and a robust building envelope assembly with outboard insulation and spray foam, providing an R-value of forty-nine. The highly compressed construction season required a short build timeline, and the project was constructed in under six months. The heavily timbered site perimeter was partially cleared years ago, so the lodge was built within the boundary of this existing clearing.

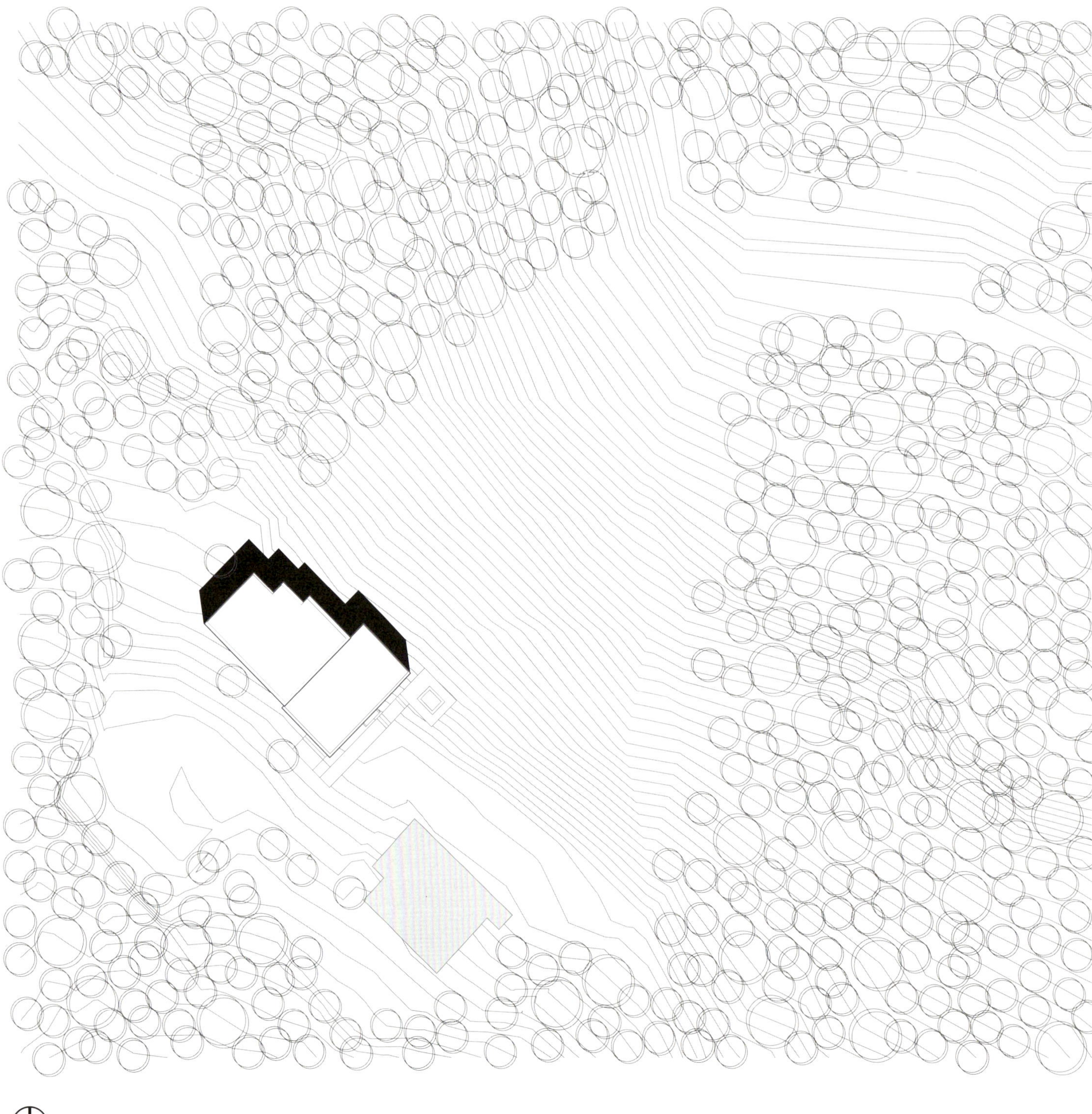

Upper Level

Main Level

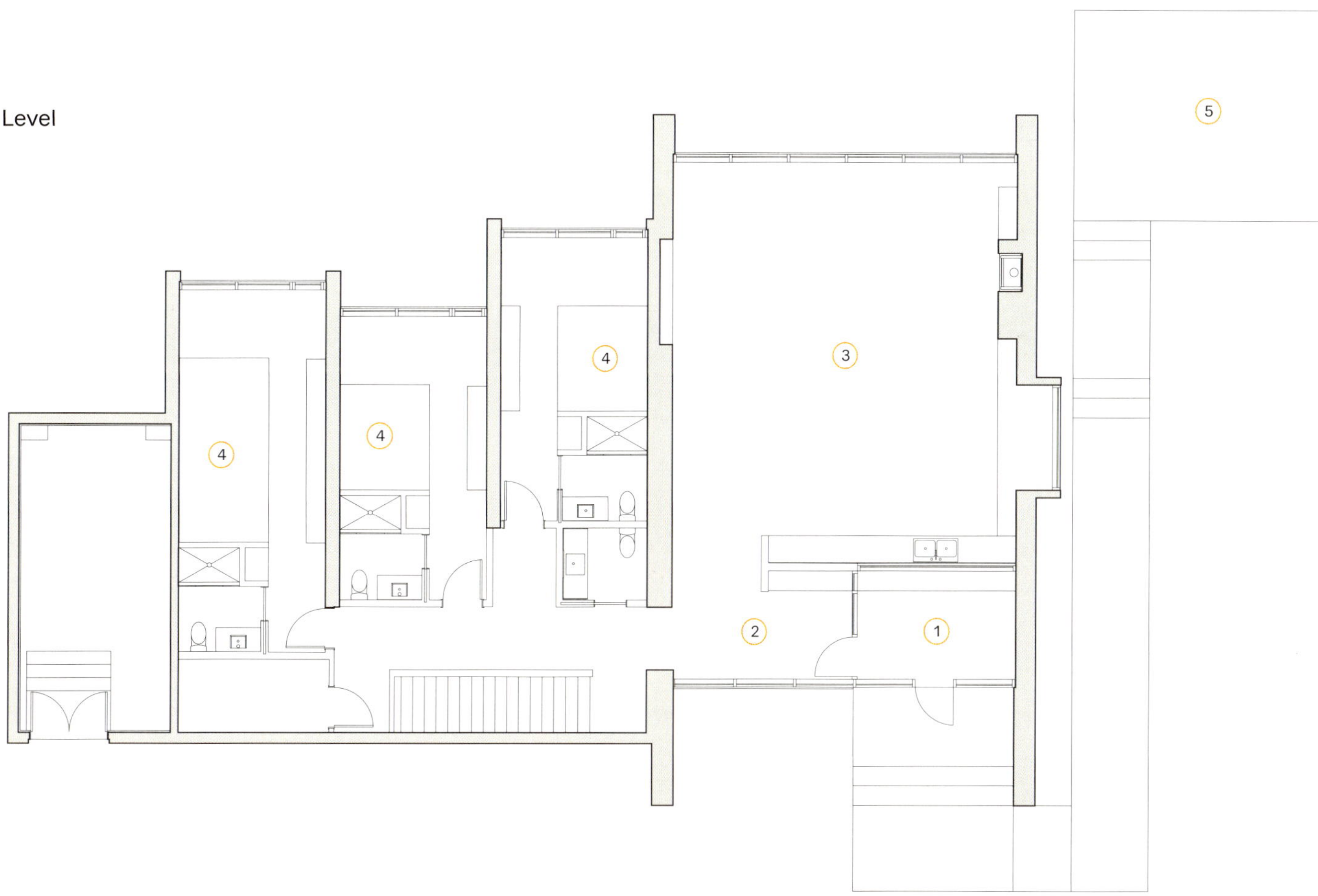

1 Entry
2 Lobby
3 Public Gathering Space
4 Guest Room
5 Spa
6 Roof Below

Image Captions		
	1	Facade detail; Hangfei Zhang
	2	Facade detail with aurora borealis; Hangfei Zhang
	3	Heuristic device
	4	North facade; Hangfei Zhang
	5	Night images of East facade with aurora borealis; Hangfei Zhang Site plan
	6	Upper-level floor plan Main-level floor plan
	7	Interior image; image courtesy of My Global USA
	8	Interior image; image courtesy of My Global USA
	9	East facade; Hangfei Zhang
	10	Facade detail; Hangfei Zhang

Completed	2019
Size	4,400 SF (409 m²)
Location	Fairbanks, Alaska
Client	My Global USA (Henry Yang and Hangfei Zhang)
Team	John Sparano Seth Striefel Anne Mooney Nate King Jun Li Morgan Birch (model)
Collaborators	Gregory Liebl (structural engineering)
General Contractor	Johnson River Enterprises

Aurora Villa

Gilb Museum of Arcadia Heritage

This municipal museum and home of the Arcadia Historical Society preserves and celebrates the city of Arcadia's diverse community and rich history. The Gilb Museum of Arcadia Heritage houses a permanent collection as well as continually rotating exhibitions depicting the history and heritage of this area of Los Angeles County. A wide range of programs and exhibits encourage community involvement in a series of flexibly designed spaces, including multipurpose rooms, exhibition galleries, storage and archival areas, curatorial spaces, and exterior exhibition spaces, including a donor courtyard and event zone.

The architecture recognizes relationships to the site and an existing community center west of the museum through geometric and material references. In this study of quiet contradiction, the museum takes its cues from the orientation of the street, the adjacent community center, and a storm-water drainage canal that separates the site from the municipal golf course.[i] The architecture absorbs these geometries to create a series of graceful, irregular spaces. The museum is urban in the way Robert Venturi, after his sojourn in Rome, suggested that buildings ought to be: acknowledging, incorporating, perhaps resolving their neighbors' discordant geometries.[ii]

The plan joins two volumes housing the museum's public and private functions, wrapped by a porous screen of sustainably harvested ipe wood louvers. The opaque volume houses services; the exhibition volume, enclosed by a porous wooden screen, is shifted in plan to form an irregular interstitial space, covered but open to the air. At the entrance, the screen is broken and folded back to welcome visitors. Clerestory windows and carefully focused openings provide controlled natural light into the galleries and offer views to the nearby San Gabriel Mountains. These views are incorporated into the exhibits as the collection's historical artifacts are juxtaposed with the view of the mountain-range backdrop framing the site. Other materials include brick, concrete masonry units, and polished concrete floors.

The process began with the development of a conceptual viewing apparatus, which explored the impact of various filters on what and how history is understood.[iii] This construct was then translated into an architecture that changes dramatically according to the position of the observer. When viewed at a right angle, the museum's wood louver facade seemingly dissolves, as one can see directly through the screen. From an oblique angle view, the facade appears as a solid surface.

The design was guided by an analysis of the complex relationship between the historian, who records and interprets the past, and the museum visitor experiencing the present.[iv] Central to this relationship is the understanding that history is accessed through secondary sources. The inevitable lens of bias, whether conscious or unconscious, filters history, which affects meaning and interpretation. To understand history, we must recognize our own relationship to the past and be aware of the curatorial editing that is ultimately presented to the public. The design of the Gilb Museum of Arcadia Heritage seeks to heighten visitors' awareness of the existence of these filters and biases. This is accomplished, in part, by dissolving traditional boundaries in the museum experience and inviting direct interaction with key aspects of the collection.

These concepts naturally extend into the development of the exhibit design, which assumes a hyper-flexible, democratic approach to showcasing the collection. The architecture, exhibits, and museum graphics were all designed and produced by the architectural team, incorporating flexible, changeable elements and continuity with the building itself. These apparatus include chalkboards for changing text, corkboard frames for rotating displays, and movable, open display cases that transform the space by their positioning, each element inviting hands-on interaction with the collection. The project was a collaboration between public and private entities, including the Gilb Family Foundation, the Arcadia Historical Society, and the city of Arcadia.

i

The city of Arcadia is renowned as the home of Santa Anita Park, a thoroughbred racetrack hosting some of the most prominent horse-racing events in the United States. The track is located a short distance from the museum site, and a portion of the collection is dedicated to the history of this iconic landmark. Arcadia is located in the San Gabriel Valley, and the museum design includes several moments in the architecture that present views of the mountain range from within the exhibition space.

ii

This description of the museum is taken, in part, from the May 2002 article written by Tim Culvahouse in *World Architecture* entitled "Lessons from History."

iii

The conceptual phase involved the design and production of a heuristic device exploring indirect and layered views. This was later translated into the building's architectural screen and informed the flexible interior exhibition design.

iv

The ideas for this historical museum and their translation into conceptual constructs, and then into architecture, were grounded in research informed, in part, by Edward Hallett Carr's book *What Is History?* (first published by Macmillan in 1961 and Penguin Books in 1964). This text is a collection of lectures Carr delivered at the University of Cambridge in 1961 on the theory of history, objectivity in historical documentation, and the role of the historian.

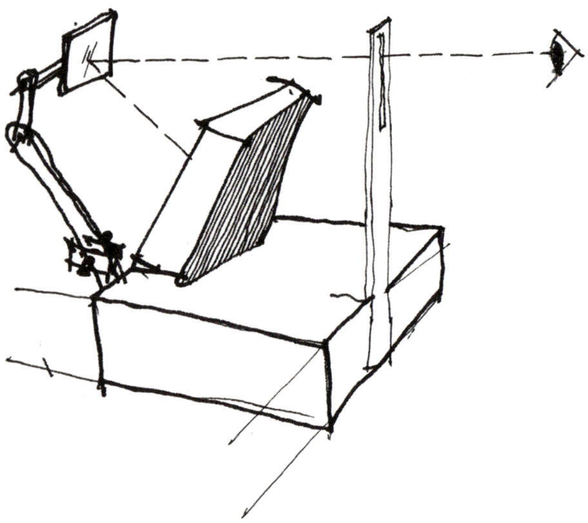

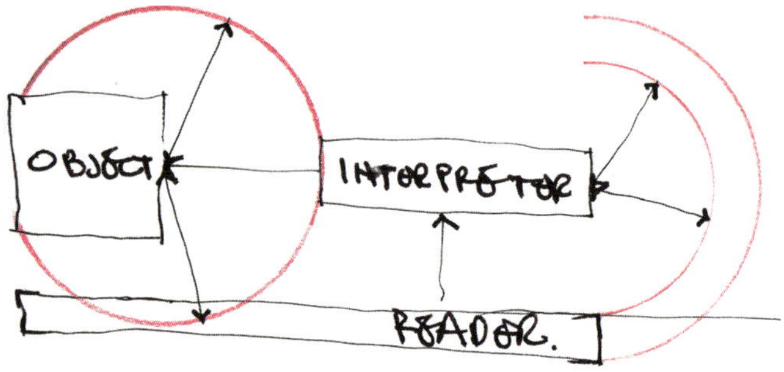
OBJECT
INTERPRETOR
READER.

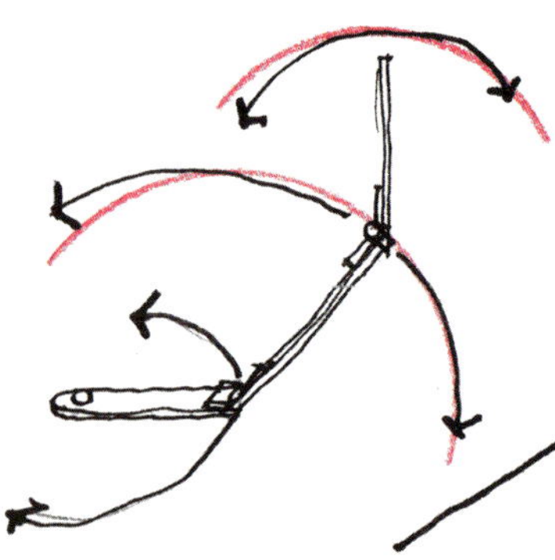

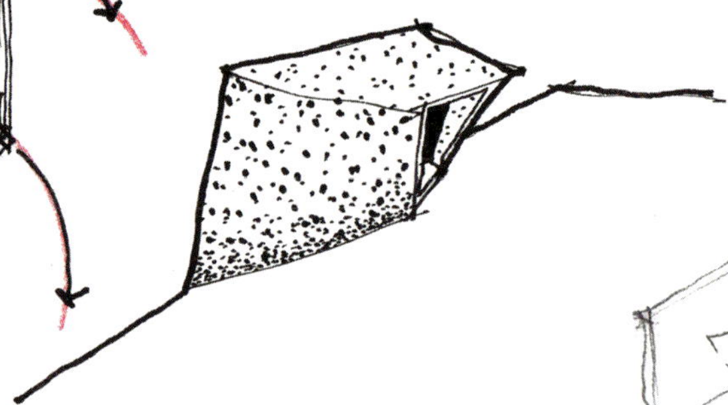

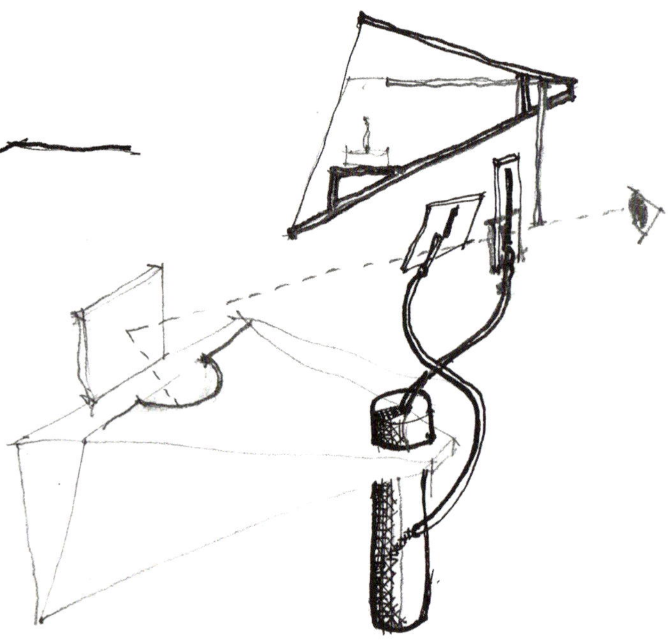

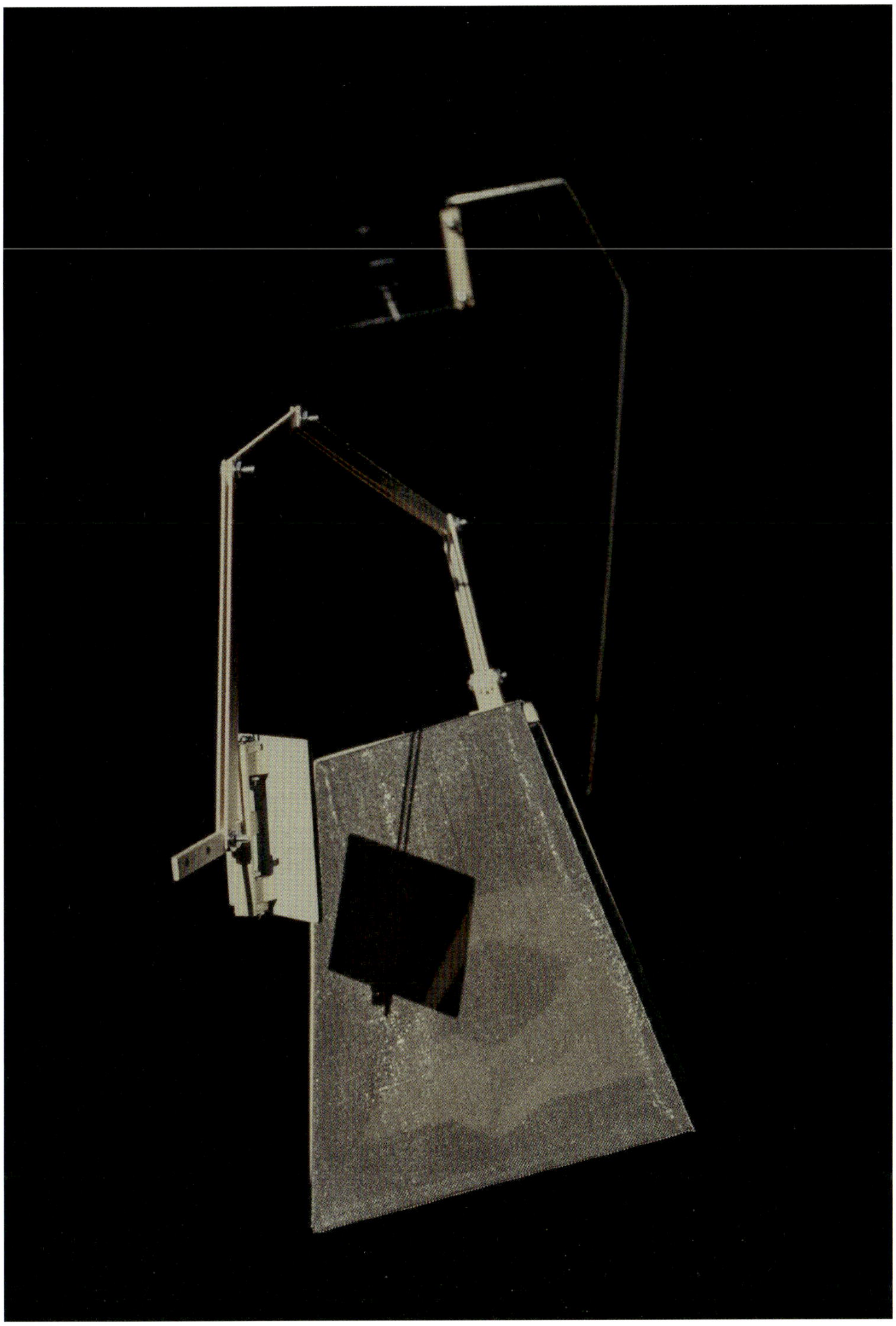

RUTH & CHARLES GILB
ARCADIA
HISTORICAL MUSEUM

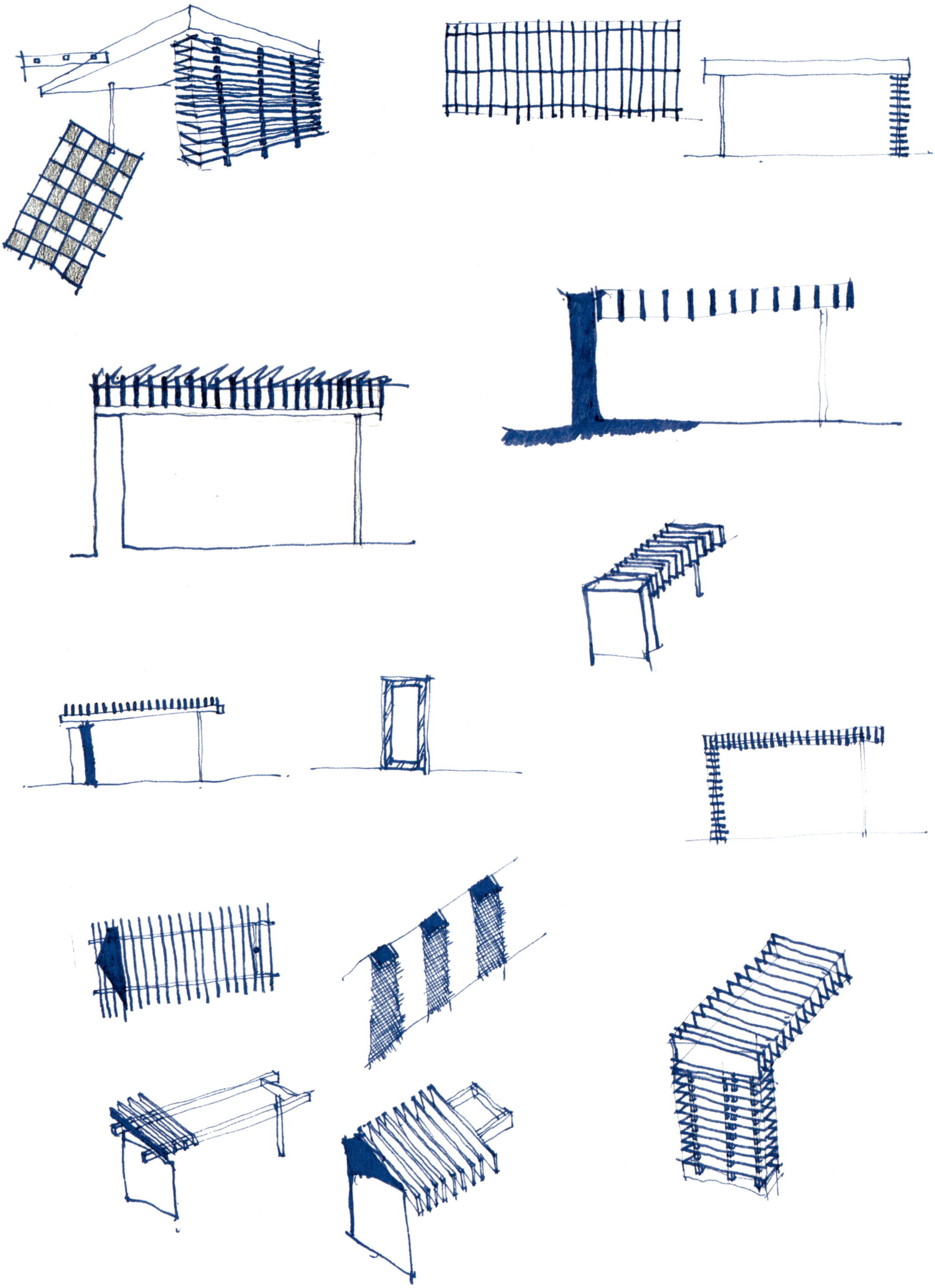

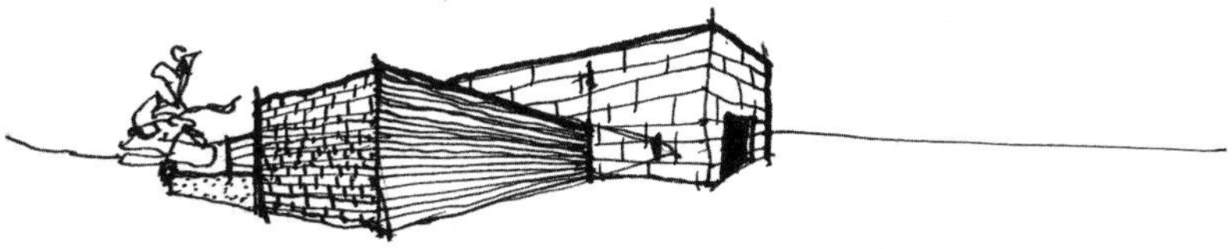

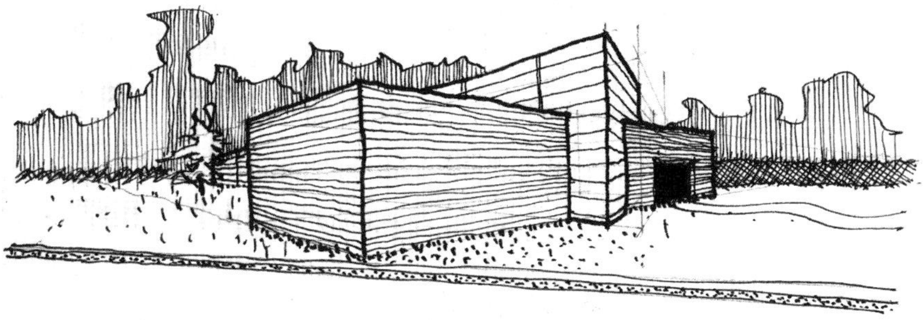

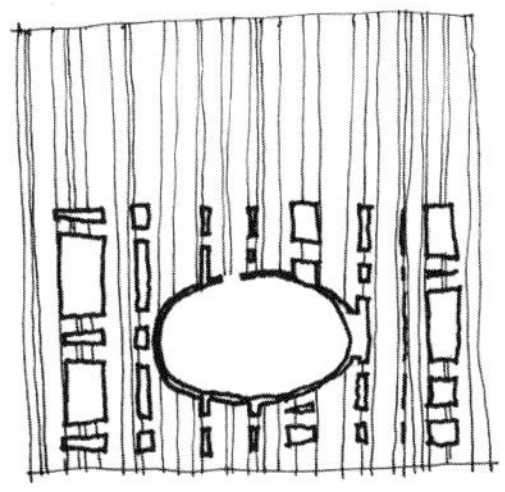

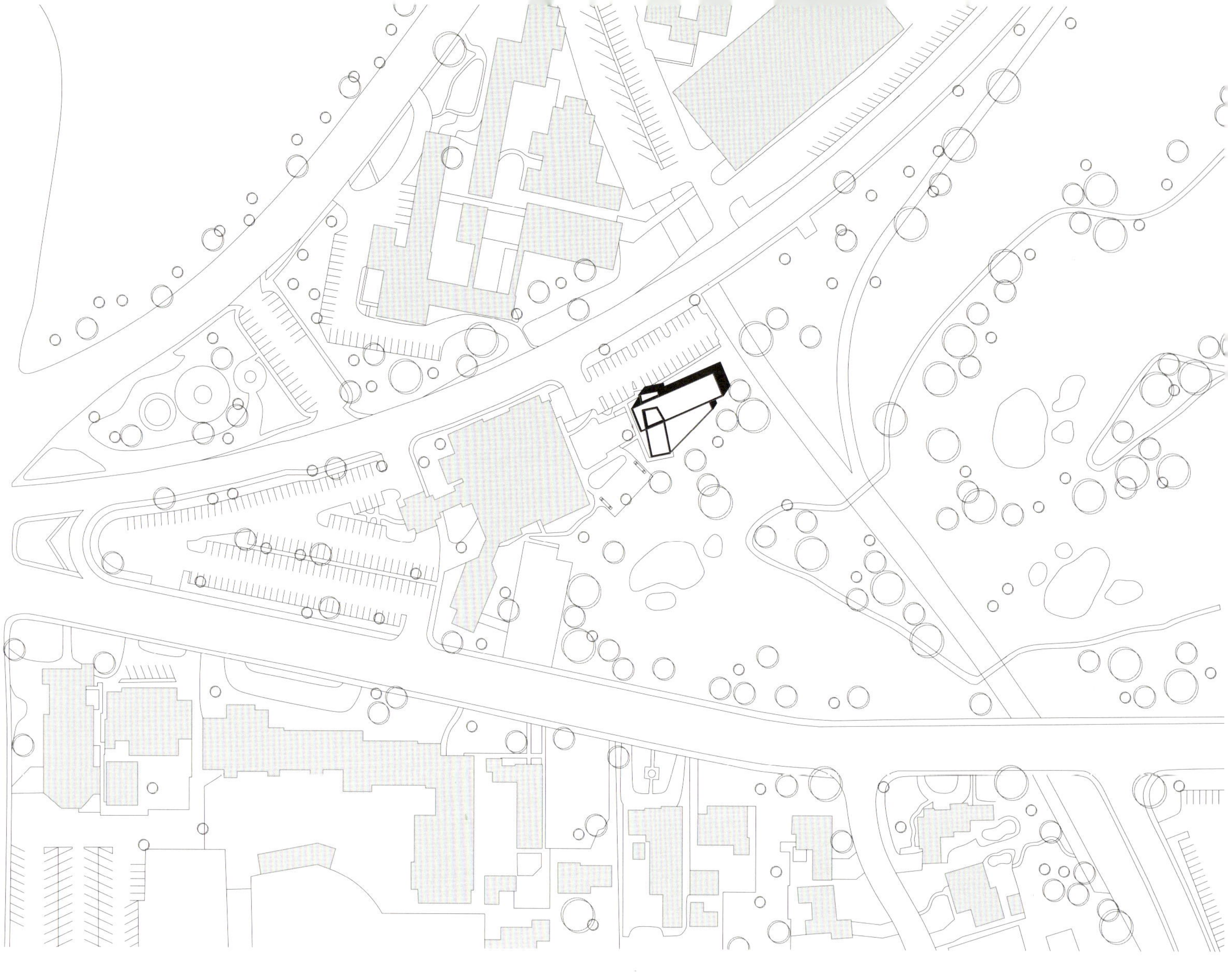

Main Level

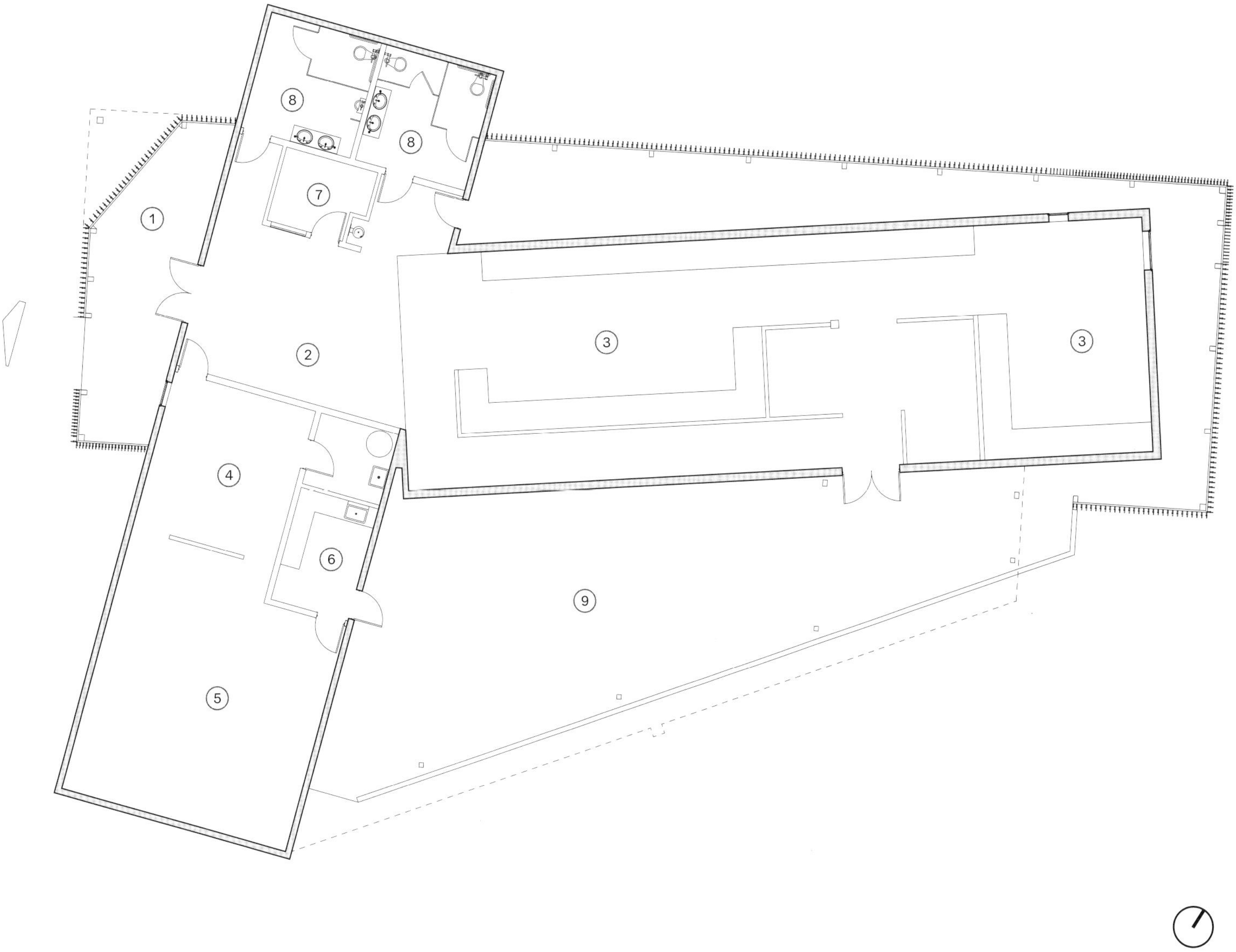

1 Entry Forecourt
2 Lobby
3 Exhibit Space
4 Meeting Room
5 Storage
6 Kitchen
7 Office
8 Restroom
9 Covered Patio Area

Image Captions		
	1	West facade (detail)
	2	Heuristic device sketches; John Sparano
	3	Heuristic device
	4	North facade; © John Linden
	5	Entry study sketches; John Sparano
	6	Massing and plan study sketches; John Sparano
	7	Detail of northwest corner; © John Linden
	8	West facade; © John Linden
	9	Site plan
		Final model
	10	Floor plan
	11	View from the northwest; © John Linden

Completed	2000
Size	4,000 SF (372 m^2)
Location	Arcadia, California
Owner	City of Arcadia, Arcadia Historical Society
Team	John Sparano Anne Mooney Michael Atkinson Matt Bean Rene Berndt Mahnaz Zahiry Ludwing Juarez Tomahisa Miyauchi (model)
Collaborators	Melisa Keeler (exhibits/graphics) Maroko & Shwe, Inc. (mechanical engineering) Silver Roth & Associates (electrical engineering) William Koh & Associates (structural engineering) Civil Trans (civil engineering) Gil Flores (landscape architecture) Jo Drummond (specifications)
General Contractor	Begel Construction

Gilb Museum of Arcadia Heritage

Hikmet Sidney Loe

CONCEPTUAL CONSTRUCTS: SPARANO + MOONEY'S INVESTIGATIVE ART OF ARCHITECTURE

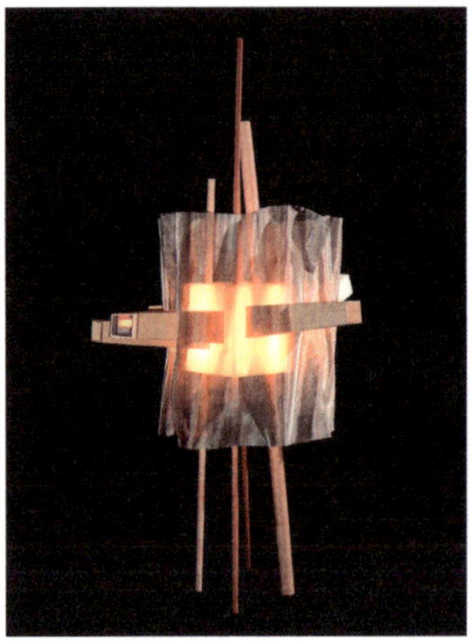

[fig. 1] Conceptual Construct, Santa Fe Springs Performing Arts Center, 2001

[fig. 2] August Fuhrmann, "A drawing of a Kaiserpanorama with 25 viewing stations," 1880. Upload by Nieborak, 2008. Licensed under {PD-1923}. Via Wikipedia Commons

A small sculptural work sits in a window well, extending from the building's facade into the space of the sidewalk (fig. 1). The piece combines wood and metal mesh, immediately calling to mind both the natural world and the world we fabricate. If the mesh started as a flat, rectangular shape, it is now wrapped around itself, belying its own materiality as it takes on a fabric-like quality. Four dowel rods of differing lengths form the core of the work, serving as the base around which the mesh appears to float. Three small, hollow wooden shapes pierce the mesh—suggesting optical viewing devices—inviting us to see the work's interior. The sculpture appears both delicate and resilient at the same time, complete through balance and poise, and created from materials representing both solid and void.

The window well is part of Sparano + Mooney's studio, a small entrée into the firm's well-ordered, bright interior where unencumbered spaces flow through each workroom. Additional sculptural works are positioned throughout, on desks, tables, and walls, each created in a process that eschews traditional boundaries often prescribed in the practice of architecture or art. Led by the firm's principals, John Sparano and Anne Mooney, these works are an integral part of their creative process. The firm describes them as "heuristic devices," from the Greek term *heuriskein*, indicating an iterative method employed for discovery.

Sparano and Mooney met while working in Los Angeles. Each was educated in cutting-edge creative processes through their respective graduate programs (Architectural Association, Columbia, and the Southern California Institute of Architecture), which they have since transformed and embraced as an integral part of the way they continue to work.[i] They employ artistic creativity to realize a built project—a unique process to design architecture. Often, architects bring assumptions and preconceptions to the design process. Sparano + Mooney's goal is to develop architecture through a unique method, which provides a framework to evaluate ideas and a mechanism for a democratic design process accessible to all employees, from interns to principals.

Art historian Rosalind Krauss's essay "Sculpture in the Expanded Field" describes the breakdown of proscribed practices and perceptions of sculpture in the 1960s and 1970s, similar to the way Sparano + Mooney works across disciplines: "It is obvious that the logic of the space of postmodernist practice is no longer organized around the definition of a given medium on the grounds of material, or, for that matter, the perception of material."[ii]

To create these conceptual constructs, the firm's team engages in a wide variety of inquiry and research, including reading, writing, sketching, and drawing, as they explore ideas in two dimensions before creating the three-dimensional forms.

The team's engagement with clients leads to further investigation and understanding of the project at hand, and its program, site, and location. Conceptualization leads to the construct, which then moves toward architectural iterations. Constructs do not typically resemble the realized project; their link is formed through the ideas embedded in these works. The firm's method sometimes results in a direct linear path from construct to realized project; other times, a meandering process occurs, akin to traveling a circuitous path.

While an invisible link binds construct to project, these compositions are also independent artworks with antecedents or influences found within the history of art, including Neolithic monuments, ancient Greek theater, and contemporary modernist sculpture. As sculptural pieces, the constructs are uniquely modern, both siteless and mobile. There is an inherent intimacy in each object, which invites handling and viewing it in the round. Wood or other natural materials often form the work. Sometimes the surface is left rough; sometimes it is exquisitely honed and crafted. Some constructs are functional; some may include text; others still are interactive.

As a body of work, distinct themes emerge, including light as actuality, illumination as metaphor, perception through spatial transitions, regional considerations, and visual art functioning as an optical device. Select constructs and their resulting architecture—including cultural centers, churches, and private residences—illustrate these themes as each construct's private sphere is projected into the public realm.

Returning to the construct in the window well (fig. 1), the viewer is invited to delve into an active, sensory experience while interacting with the work. The importance of sight becomes apparent as each of the three wooden "windows" affords a different perspective into the work's center. A historical precedent for this work is found in the nineteenth century, when public viewing apparatuses became increasingly accessible through advances in optical devices.

The German inventor August Fuhrmann invented the Kaiser-Panorama, a large-scale circular viewing station that enabled multiple visitors the means to view stereoscopic images, a precursor to the camera. As seen in the drawing of the Kaiser-Panorama with twenty-five viewing stations (fig. 2), audiences "would simultaneously be viewing different stereoscopic images illuminated by 25 small lamps. The interior contained a motor that rotated the slides at roughly two-minute intervals from viewer to viewer."[iii] Even if surrounded by other visitors, staring into the Kaiser-Panorama was a singular activity: the exterior world fell away as the viewer's focus narrowed into an interior world, similar to experiencing this construct.

Sculptural works operating as viewing devices find notable examples in the Land Art movement. Many of these monumental sculptures call attention to site—and sight—leading to a breakdown in the assumed absolutes that defined both sculpture and architecture. American artist Nancy Holt's earthwork *Sun Tunnels* (1973–76; fig. 3)—formed by four concrete pipes laid in an "X" pattern in Utah's West Desert—operates as a viewing mechanism of a desert landscape, changed through constant alterations of light and atmospheric phenomena. Holt describes the panoramic view as "too overwhelming to take in without visual reference points."[iv] She continues, "The view blurs out rather than sharpens. Through the tunnels, parts of the landscape are framed and come into focus."[v] As visitors to *Sun Tunnels* consider Holt's sculptural form as a viewing device in the landscape, we turn back to Sparano + Mooney's constructs and find shared similarities with earthworks through materiality, form, and intention.

Visual access, both seen and unseen, is exemplified in the conceptual construct illustrated in figure 4. Resting on the table at three different points, it is seemingly

[fig. 3] Nancy Holt, *Sun Tunnels*, 1973-76. Great Basin Desert, Utah. Dia Art Foundation with support from Holt/Smithson Foundation. © Holt/Smithson Foundation and Dia Art Foundation/VAGA at Artists Rights Society (ARS), NY. Photo: Hikmet Sidney Loe

[fig. 4] Conceptual Construct, Gilb Museum of Arcadia Heritage, 1998

fragile in its ability to tilt or tip. The candle at its center symbolizes an event. The main visual access to the candle is through a screen on one axis of the device, which acts as a metaphorical filter to both physical and visual access. On the opposite side of that same access, a small aperture offers the possibility of viewing the candle. Above this opening is a suspended viewer, while behind the viewer is a mirror, trained on the screen that filters the candle.

There is a strong correlation between this construct and the ideas posited within Greek philosopher Plato's work "Allegory of the Cave." Each investigation offers an interpretation of light and ideas. Plato's dialogue describes a scene where people are bound inside a cave, limited to seeing what is directly in front of them. A fire illuminates their interior world, while a wall crosses their sight line where people pass, "carrying all sorts of vessels, and statues and figures of animals made of wood and stone and various materials."[vi] With sight limited, the cave dweller's reality is informed by shadows. This optical experience, with forms statically presented to viewers, is akin to the construct that marries light and sight in the physical world.

The perception of the world around us, illuminated (or not), correlates to the ideas of curatorial practices of interpretation. This construct was one creative way the firm worked to realize the built project the Gilb Museum of Arcadia Heritage, dedicated to regional history and located in greater Los Angeles. To progress from idea to construct to realized project, the project's team first reread Edward Hallett Carr's pivotal publication *What Is History?*, mining the relationship of historian to history to understand the role of the museum curator, who controls what the public accesses in a museum setting. Carr, alluding to this role, explains, "History therefore is a process of selection in terms of historical significance ... and the standard of historical significance is his ability to fit them into his pattern of rational explanation and interpretation."[vii]

The firm's project drew elements from the construct and the design process. The building is wrapped by a porous structure of vertical wooden slats set parallel to each other. Depending on the visitor's situation to the building's exterior, the structure appears as a solid mass or a porous screen allowing access to the facade. The visitor's position to the building determines view and perception, referencing ideas embodied in the construct. The construct's embedded candle transcends ocular necessity to serve as a metaphor for illumination, both felt and seen as a continual presence.

Themes of light—from illumination to the metaphor of enlightenment—unite many of the practice's conceptual constructs, while natural light, ambient light,

[fig. 5] Conceptual Construct, Saint Joseph the Worker Catholic Church, 2009

[fig. 6] Kurt Schwitters, *To the Prince of Siberia*, 1924. Pencil, ink, pastel, and printed collage, 9.3 x 8.9 in (23.6 x 22.7 cm). AM81-65-893. Musée National d'Art Moderne, Centre Georges Pompidou, Paris, France. © CNAC/MNAM, Dist. RMN-Grand Palais/Art Resource, NY. Photo: Jacques Faujour

[fig. 7] Conceptual Construct, Design Competition Entry for the Cathedral of Our Lady of the Assumption, Port-au-Prince, Haiti, 2013

and candlelight serve to codify space (fig. 5). This conceptual construct references candles situated in churches, their shape, materiality, and spiritual references. The realized project Saint Joseph the Worker Catholic Church takes its oval shape from the construct, reflecting the participatory nature elicited through the rounded form. The wooden dowel was worked in wax, and these wax segments then turn on the interior dowel. With the turn of the dowel, figures appear, change, recombine, and take on new meaning.

The construct's interactive nature helps us understand the relationships of the different figures, such as Saint Joseph and an ordinary man holding a child. Action and engagement become metaphors for active participation in sacred experiences. Discussions centered on the role of this church and a desire to create sacred space that is not passive but instead reflective of conscious participation through the action of worship.

The construct's themes of spirituality and its materiality of wood are enhanced by the use of collage. Aspects of collage also become metaphor, marrying different elements and materials to create a new work that transcends its parts toward a newly envisioned whole. The artistic practice of collage finds origins in the Spanish artist Pablo Picasso's early twentieth-century works. Other artists, including German artist Kurt Schwitters, quickly adopted this practice and made it their own, as in Schwitters' 1924 work *To the Prince of Siberia* (fig. 6).

Light and the modification of optical devices are a few of the themes embedded in the conceptual construct created while considering a cathedral in Haiti (fig. 7). The piece was created by deconstructing a camera (an optical apparatus), then casting its parts in beeswax. The wooden construct allows viewers to look at the camera pieces, illuminated through the wax. The device as camera, and the deconstructed camera, become metaphors for the cathedral as each captures light, holding its rays and lending warmth. The experience of light and the abstraction of its qualities are found in both cathedral and construct. Light is not about dogma; it is about illumination.

Beeswax is the base material used to create encaustic: beeswax (or other resins or oils) is heated, then pigment is added, binding to form a painterly substance. The paint is thick and malleable, rendering it ideal for more sculptural works and the addition of objects. From first-century BCE Romano-Egyptian mummy portraits to early Christian icons to the paintings of American artist Jasper Johns and sculptures of German artist Wolfgang Laib, encaustic has been used for its unique binding properties and luminescence.

[fig. 8] Conceptual Construct, Santa Fe Springs Performing Arts Center, 2001

The small, industrial Southern California town of Santa Fe Springs commissioned Sparano + Mooney Architecture to design a performing arts center next to a park with sports fields. Sports and performing arts are both enacted on a stage. Each requires practice, yet the outcome varies as the event takes place in real time. The historical antecedent for these activities can be found staged in a clearing in the forest. In these primitive gathering spaces, through the heaviness of surrounding trees, their density forms a natural delineation between daily human activity and the supernatural world of performance.

The relationship between sports and the performing arts led the firm to A. Bartlett Giamatti's 2011 book *Take Time for Paradise: Americans and Their Games.*[viii] These ideas led to a construct based upon nonhierarchical approaches to the object (fig. 8). The device includes multiple openings focused on a contained view, serving as a three-dimensional viewing device. One viewpoint proffers a semblance to a Greek dance; another contains a mirror, offering a reflection back to oneself as subjective viewer of the performance. A third perspective includes an endless reflection.

Translating the device into architecture brought many elements of the construct to the realized site for the Santa Fe Springs Performing Arts Center. The design offers entrances on each side; trees surround the center, harkening back to the central clearing amid the forest for performative events. Skylights grace the building, allowing light from above, while perforations in the building's facade bring dappled light into the interior, as found in a copse or forest. Both interior and exterior spaces are used for performances and events.

This construct, with columns surrounding the center, is reminiscent of one of Swiss artist Alberto Giacometti's more enigmatic works, *The Palace at 4 a.m.* (1932-33; fig. 9). Giacometti describes this multimedia piece that exudes intimacy:

> *For many years I have executed only sculptures that have presented themselves to my mind entirely completed. I have limited myself to reproducing them in space without changing anything, without asking myself what they could mean. ... The attempts to which I have sometimes given way, of conscious realization of a picture or even a sculpture, have always failed.*[ix]

The architectural aspect of this sculpture is found in its definition of space, delineated and defined by the creatures inhabited within its structure.

The point of departure for the Emigration Canyon Residence was the idea of family as a fluid, dynamic construct. A family, comprised of various ages and relationships, is

[fig. 9] Alberto Giacometti, *The Palace at 4 a.m.*, 1932–33. Construction in wood, glass, wire, and string, 25 x 28 1/4 x 15 3/4 in (63.5 x 71.8 x 40 cm). Purchase. 90.1936. DIGITAL IMAGE © 2021 The Museum of Modern Art/Scala, Florence

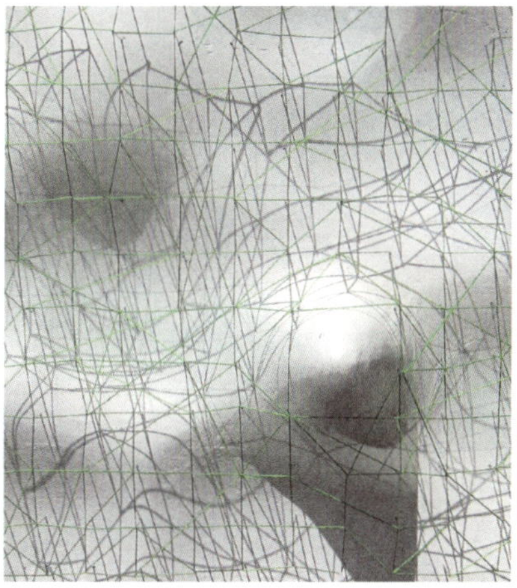

[fig. 10] Conceptual Construct, Emigration Canyon Residence, 2010

[fig. 11] Entrance to Newgrange, County Meath, Ireland. Upload by spudmurphy, 2009. Licensed under {PD-1923}. Via Wikipedia Commons

the opposite of a static entity. The conceptual construct reflects this web of interconnectivity as a network of string floating above an undulating base, a dynamic topography (fig. 10). The string is strong but also fragile, a metaphor for a family's history. There is an order, a pattern to the web, but it is also chaotic, representative of life. Both life within the family and life outside, in the world, directly impact the nature of this structure.

These ideas reappear in the realized architecture. The use of Corten steel as cladding for the residence embodies many aspects of the family: the exterior of the home is akin to skin, and at first, it is a reflective surface that acquires its patina over time—the vulnerability of the material becomes its strength. The simple form of the house includes three solid sides to the volume, with the fourth side open with a seventy-foot curtain covering its windows. The theatrical reference to people and their roles, coming and going behind the curtain, alludes to the house as a stage, as does the harlequin pattern of the exterior cladding. This references the construct's web and finds similar patterning throughout history in many ages and civilizations, including the Celtic triskelion knot depicted at the entrance of Newgrange, the prehistoric passage tomb in County Meath, Ireland (fig. 11). Swirling together yet distinctly individual, each aspect of the knot can be understood as a family member or elements of a home embedded in its site.

Another private residence, Glashausen, is also located in Emigration Canyon. The property is overwhelming on many levels: it is large enough to encompass historic sheep trails, grazing areas, and game trails left by moose, deer, and other creatures. Hikers and mountain bikers now also intersect the property. The natural world proffers an infinite spectrum of design opportunities, which allowed additional ideas to enter into the process. The owner is employed in the digital world, maintaining a global orientation between Utah and Switzerland. His desire to situate a minimalistic house amid nature's grandeur led to the creation of this project's conceptual construct.

The architects took a stone from the property and encased it in layers of plexiglass, referencing the digital, human-made world. The resulting construct is a cube approximately four inches on each side (fig. 12). The stone forms an organic-shaped void inside the engineered, perfectly structured but malleable cube. Within the cube, more easily noticeable in certain light, is a double helix created by etching the binary code of the two cities the client calls home in Utah and Switzerland, along with the geographic coordinates of these places.

The inclusion of the stone allows the architecture to speak to the unmanipulated qualities of the natural world while the clear plexiglass, routed out to create a void accepting the stone, refers to the highly manipulated, designed realm of the

[fig. 12] Conceptual Construct, Glashausen, 2015

[fig. 13] Jackie Winsor, *Burnt Piece*, 1977-78. Cement, burnt wood, and wire mesh, 33 7/8 x 34 x 34 in (86 x 86.4 x 86.4 cm). Gift of Agnes Gund. 90.1991. Digital Image © The Museum of Modern Art/Licensed by SCALA/ Art Resource, NY

digital. The thin gap between the two is where the project lives conceptually. These ideas, then translated to developing the residence as natural and architectural worlds, endlessly reference each other: nature is held in the center of the home's landscaped courtyard, surrounded by the highly manipulated materials of architectural concrete, glass, and steel.

The history of Minimalist art can be read as centered on the cube: the clarity of this geometry began to appear during the 1960s. American artist Tony Smith's work *Die* was first made as a cardboard model in 1962, then fabricated in steel in 1968. His six-foot cube is impenetrable, a seemingly solid mass that confronts us with the same view on each of its visible sides. The Minimalist cube quickly became an artistic touchstone to emulate or translate anew. American artist Jackie Winsor reinterpreted the cube in several works, most notably in *Burnt Piece* (1977-78; fig. 13). Created with cement, burnt wood and mesh, Winsor invites our gaze to consider the inside of the cube. Themes of interior and exterior resonate, albeit through different materials and intentions, between Winsor's work and the Glashausen cube.

Unique in the world of architecture, Sparano + Mooney links the realms of poetry, art, and architecture, as conceptual constructs play pivotal roles in the firm's journey toward its design development. Each construct is complex, as an invisible thread runs from these works to the realized project, linking the physicality of the studio's process to embedded intellectual, environmental, and aesthetic considerations. Their complexity, along with the materiality and exquisite craft, makes them accomplished, artistic bodies of work. A keen sense of attention to the materiality of the construct is one key to the success of these pieces. Clients rarely see the constructs that guided the architects to their realized project, and viewers will naturally understand these works differently than the design team who created them. Yet, through differences of perception, each construct offers a set of multidimensional ideas and themes with which to engage both art and architecture.

Notes

i. Conversations with Anne Mooney and John Sparano in 2018 form the basis of this essay.

ii. Rosalind Krauss, "Sculpture in the Expanded Field," October 8 (Spring 1979), 43.

iii. Jonathan Crary, *Suspensions of Perception: Attention, Spectacle, and Modern Culture* (Cambridge, MA: MIT Press, 1999), 136.

iv. Nancy Holt, "Sun Tunnels," *Artforum* 15, no. 1 (April 1977), 35.

v. Holt, "Sun Tunnels," 35.

vi. Plato, "Allegory of the Cave," *Republic*, Book VII, 224.

vii. Edward Hallett Carr, *What Is History?* (New York: Alfred A. Knopf, 1964), 138.

viii. A. Bartlett Giamatti, *Take Time for Paradise: Americans and Their Games* (New York: Bloomsbury, 2011).

ix. "Alberto Giacometti: The Palace at 4 a.m.," Museum of Modern Art website (accessed January 2, 2018), http://www.moma.org/collection/works/80928.

Glashausen

The Glashausen project is a new home and 120-acre development located minutes from downtown Salt Lake City in Utah's Rocky Mountains. The site consists of a large expanse of mountainous terrain at the upper end of a canyon. The topography features a steep ridgeline covered in a mix of native Gambel oak, sage, and grasses nestled between mountain peaks. The site is home to a diverse range of wildlife and was planned to provide a protected habitat for elk, moose, and deer, and a sanctuary for birds.[i]

The goals for the project include master planning the site with a private retreat for the owners and their net-zero-energy home,[ii] as well as public zones offering all-season recreation access for hikers, cyclists, and cross-country skiers. A global client with a local base commissioned the project, and the client and architects collectively questioned the possibilities of architecture and site in a digital age that frequently emphasizes placelessness. The project also examines the role of the natural world in a digitally focused era by providing a sensory-based experience to balance the more virtual and abstract environments of the global workplace.[iii]

The house grows from the site, folding nature into the center of its minimal concrete form and carefully integrating the architecture within its wooded canyon surroundings. The plan, organized around an open courtyard concept, allows nature to flow into its center. This approach preserves the site's foreground, leaving an intact meadow and an entrance providing glimpses through the site, with the architecture framing distant views. The volume is composed of concrete and glass, highly refined, engineered, and designed with precision. The architecture sits in silent contrast to the wilderness, constantly in flux with light and shadow, wind, rain, snow, and sun.

The project offers a modern retreat from the chaos and frenetic speed of global life, and celebrates the pivotal role nature has in grounding domestic life. Interior and exterior spaces are connected through expansive glass walls, and spatial quality is achieved through the consideration of scale and proportions, materials and details. The program elements of both the main house and the guesthouse are connected under a singular roof structure. At the center of this roof is a shared courtyard with steps leading to a pool. These outdoor spaces provide a point of prospect oriented both to the sky and to distant city views.

The architecture seeks responsible development within the threshold of urban and pristine. It provides an escape for members of this family to immerse themselves in the natural amenities of their mountain property with minimal disturbance to existing conditions. The challenge of building for silence within a world filled with noise provided a compelling direction for design. Sounds on the site come from the wind rustling through leaves and the birds each morning. The architects sought to produce architecture that was quiet in its presence, incorporating systems that were also silent and did not distract from the experience of living in nature. LEED Platinum certification is targeted for the home, and it is powered by solar panels and rechargeable battery-generated energy.

i

A master plan of the entire site was performed in collaboration with the landscape architecture team Design Workshop from Aspen, Colorado. This effort involved research into the history of the site and its canyon context, and incorporated public access trails. A wildlife preserve is also included with watering holes and nesting posts for the wide variety of species found in the area.

ii

A net-zero-energy home produces enough renewable energy to power the annual energy consumption required by the home and its building systems. In this case, the architecture incorporates both active renewable energy systems and passive design strategies, including a super-insulated building envelope, high-performance window systems, and siting strategies to maximize the solar orientation, climate, and views.

iii

The conceptual device guiding the design process was a digitally manufactured enclosure for a stone found on the site. The rock was scanned and digitized to cut the layers of its plexiglass enclosure. A double helix surrounds the stone with the GPS coordinates of the client's home base in Switzerland intertwined with the coordinates of this site in Utah.

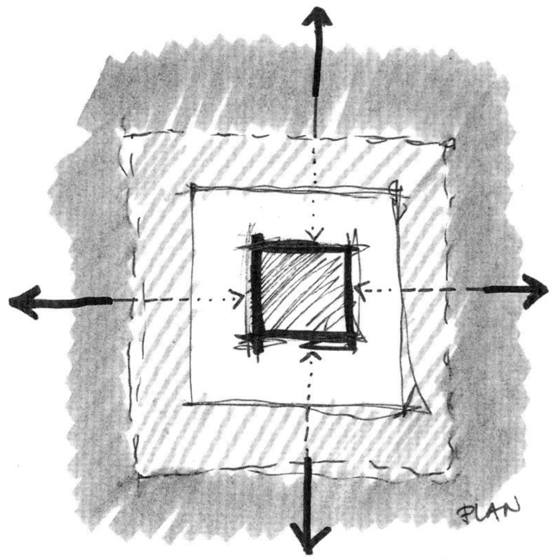
PLAN

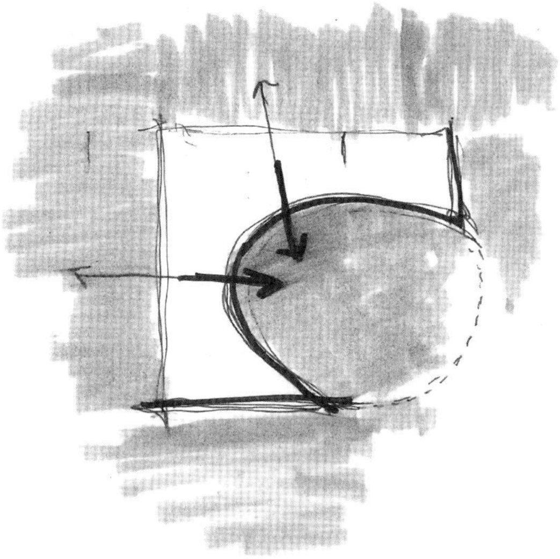

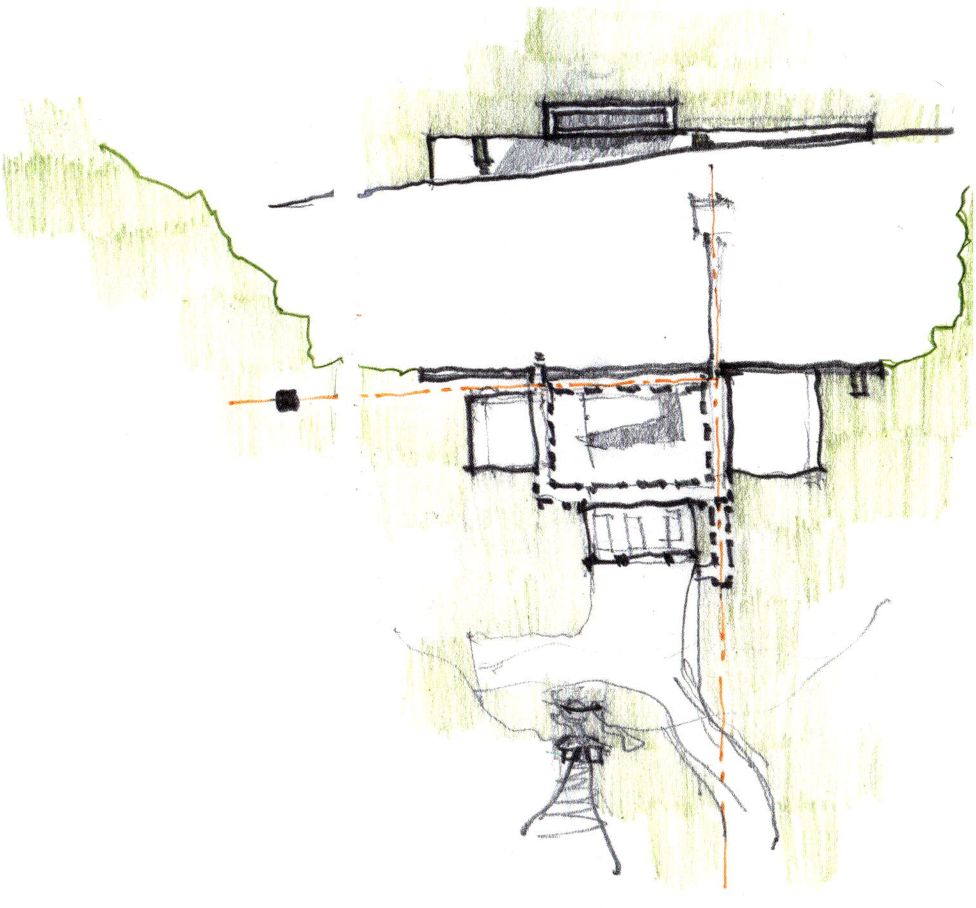

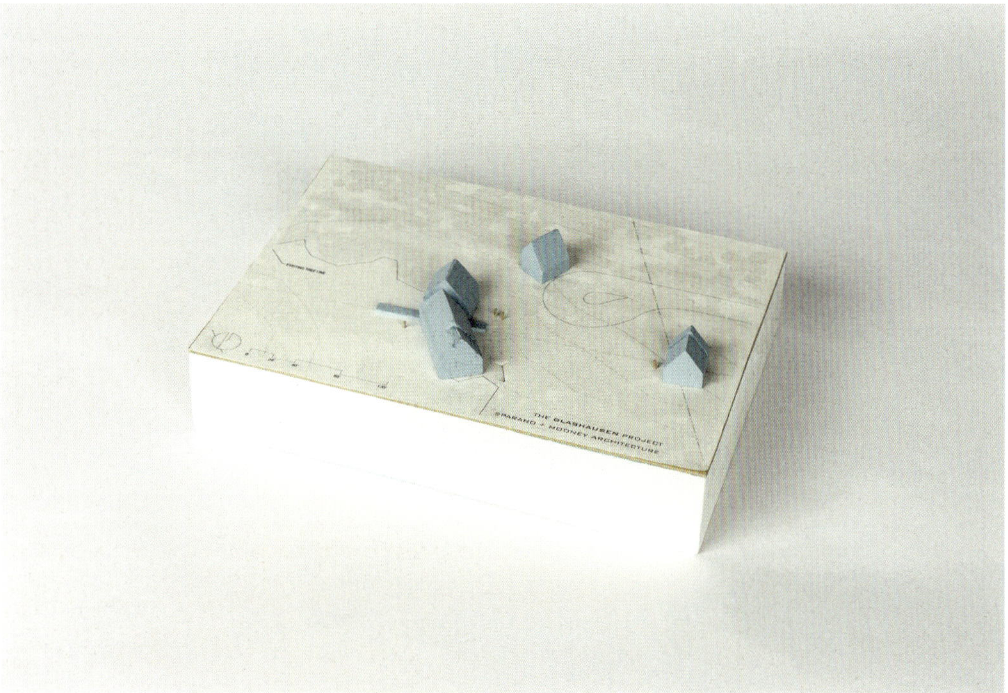
THE GLASHAUSEN PROJECT
SPARANO + MOONEY ARCHITECTURE

THE GLASHAUSEN PROJECT
SPARANO + MOONEY ARCHITECTURE

THE GLASHAUSEN PROJECT
SPARANO + MOONEY ARCHITECTURE

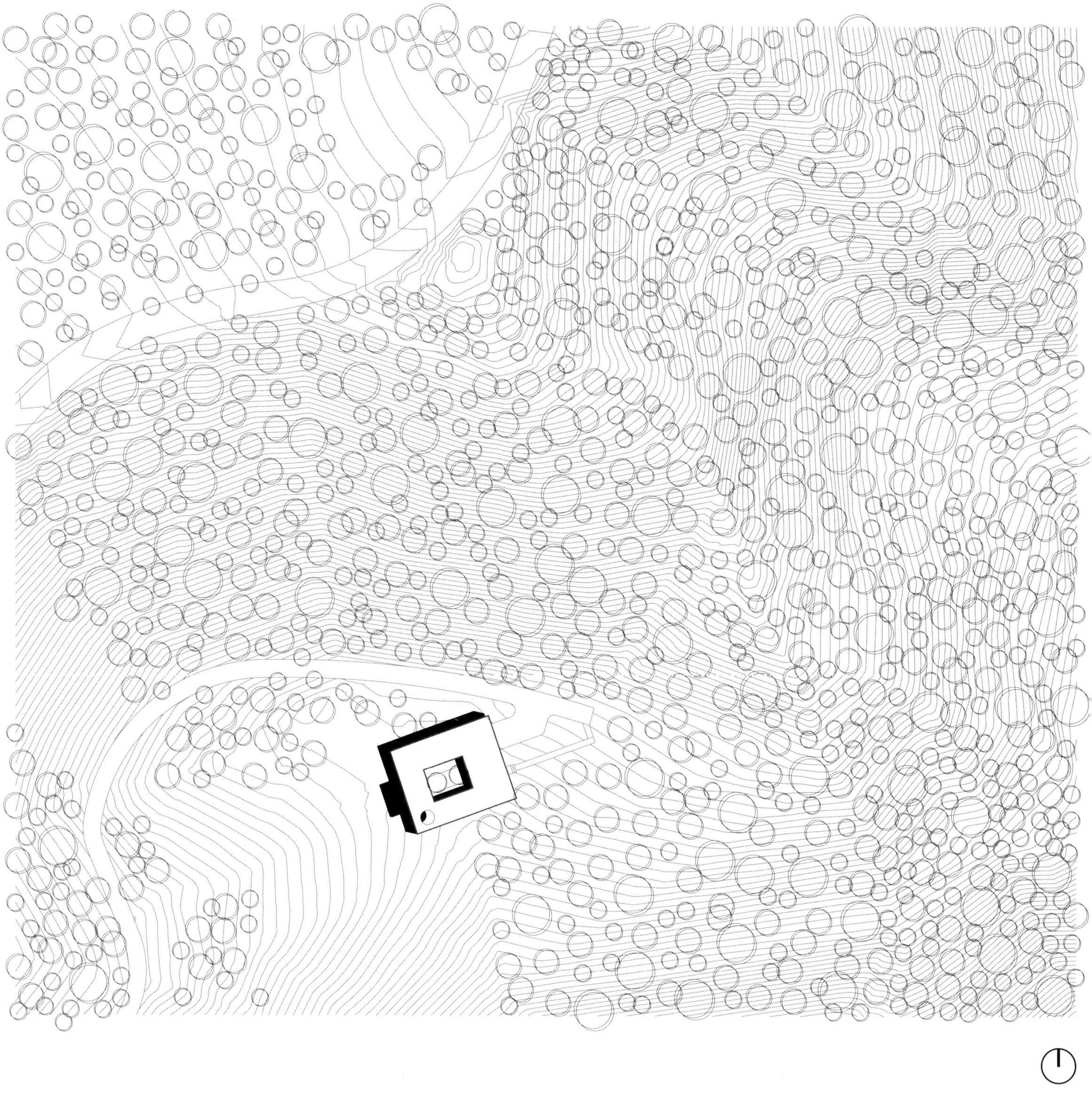

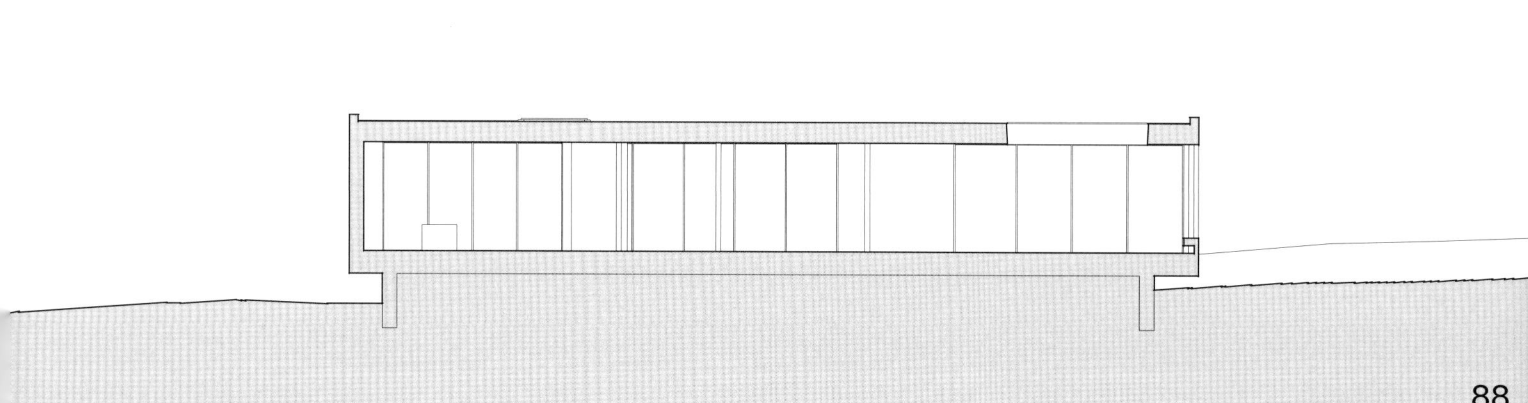

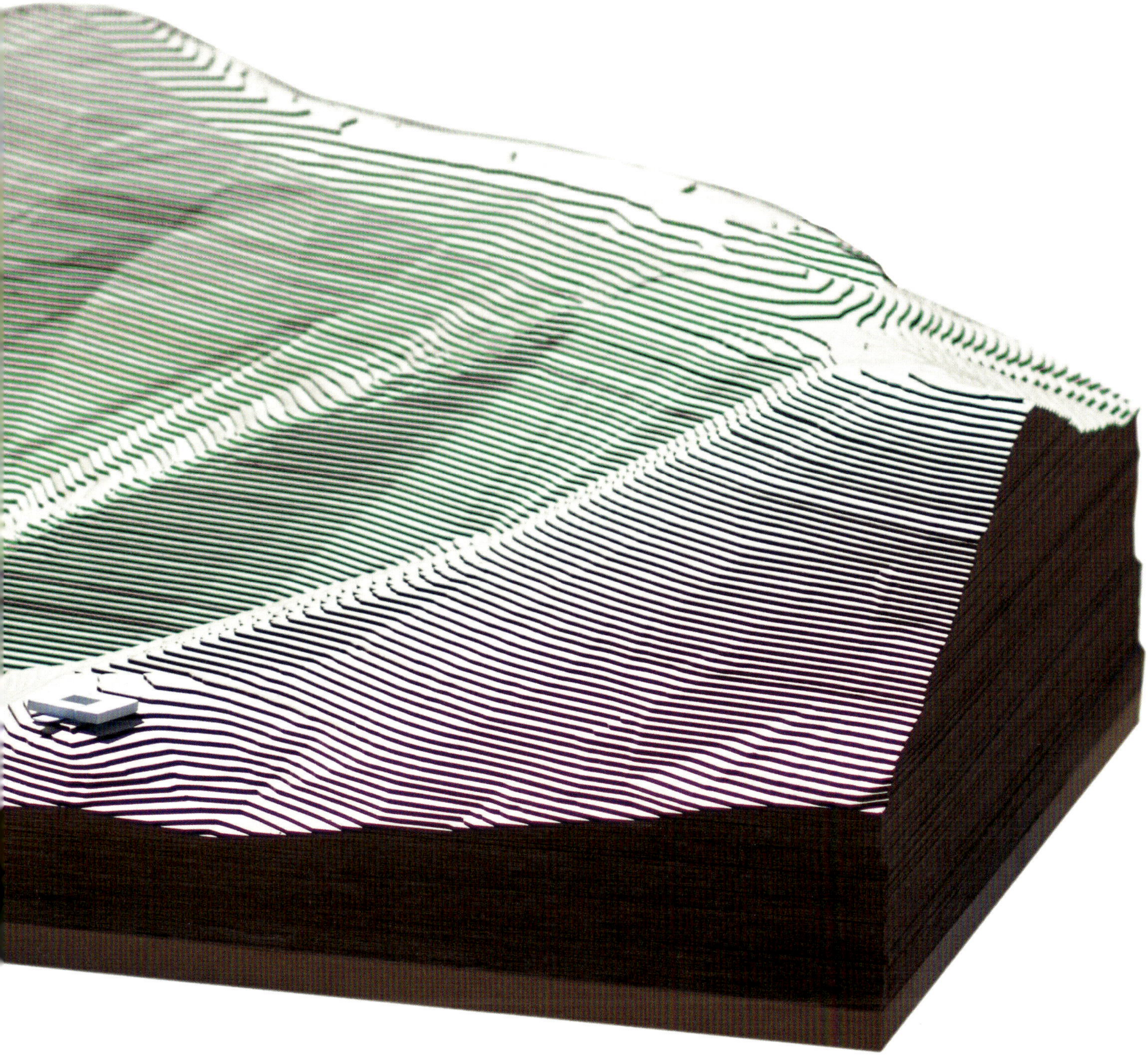

Image Captions

1	Site photo
2	Site photo Heuristic device, perspective view
3	Site photo Heuristic device, side view
4	Site photo Site photo
5	Concept sketches; John Sparano
6	Concept sketches; John Sparano
7	Concept sketches; John Sparano
8	Massing study models
9	Final model, aerial view (detail)
10	Site plan Building section
11	Exterior renderings
12	Final model, aerial view
13	Site model photo
14	Courtyard rendering Exterior rendering

Completed	2023 (anticipated)
Size	6,200 SF (576 m²)
Location	Emigration Canyon, Utah
Team	John Sparano Anne Mooney Seth Striefel Pingting Wei Ethan Zagorec-Marks
Collaborators	Structural Design Studio (structural engineering) McNeil Engineering (civil engineers)
General Contractor	Sausage

Topaz Museum

Topaz Museum and Education Center is an eight-thousand-square-foot cultural facility providing information and interpretation regarding the internment of more than eleven thousand Japanese Americans during World War II at the Topaz Internment Camp, located nearby in rural Delta, Utah. The museum includes a large exhibit space that tells the story of Topaz, organized along a chronological timeline of events during wartime nationally and in the American internment camps. One of the primary goals of the project was to provide a secure home for the museum collection, comprised of over a thousand artifacts from the camp, preserving the collection for future generations.

The exhibition was curated to engage and educate the public both about the site and the broad subject of internment. It includes interpretive panels with historical perspectives, photographs, cutting-edge interactive digital installations, collected art and artifacts, and a scale model of the camp. Highlights of the collection include poetry, shell art, painting, jewelry, and furniture representing a wealth of creative work produced with the limited materials available.[i] The exhibit space also contains a full-scale, historically accurate reconstruction of one of the housing barracks. After experiencing the interior spaces of the museum, visitors exit the building through a thirty-six-hundred-square-foot courtyard featuring a restored recreation hall salvaged from the original camp.

The location of the Topaz Museum along Delta's main thoroughfare provides maximum visibility for travelers through the state visiting the camp or nearby Great Basin National Park. The museum experience invites visitors to tour the remains of the Topaz Internment Camp site, located approximately sixteen miles northwest of the museum. The camp was closed at the end of World War II, and the buildings were eventually sold in 2007.[ii] The site was later designated a National Historic Landmark as consciousness surrounding these deeply troubling events was being raised. Today, evidence of the camp includes remnants of walkways, gardens, a gridded road network, concrete foundations for the barracks, and other artifacts.

The *parti* for the building involved linking five key spaces along a single procession of light and darkness. The experience begins at the building's entry, with low, dark ceilings and walls of charred cypress cladding; it then moves inside to a lobby and reception area, opening up to high ceilings and bright white walls, flooded with diffused northern light. Visitors then enter a transitional space, moving through a gradient shifting from light to shadow. As they move toward the darkened exhibition areas, controlled artificial light illuminates the sequence of exhibitions and artifacts. The experience terminates in an outdoor courtyard bathed in natural light with views of the vast western sky above.

The modest palette of architectural materials includes honed concrete masonry units, alluding to the relentless grid of the camp, black-charred cypress wood cladding, inspired by the traditional Japanese *shou sugi ban* process of treating wood, and polished concrete floors.[iii] The masonry blocks provide a sense of modularity and gridded order. Collectively, the materials reference the austere palette of the original buildings at the Topaz site, once comprised of black tar-paper roofs, simple uninsulated pine walls, Masonite flooring, and un-taped, unfinished, square-edge sheetrock.

i

Artists including Chiura Obata, Kay Sekimachi, Willie Ito, Miyoko Ito, Hisako Shimizu Hibi, and George Matsusaburo Hibi were inmates at Topaz, producing notable works of art in a variety of mediums during their lifetimes. An art school was formed by the internees to support creative activity and provide education and training for youth. Works of literature and poetry documented the experience of Topaz by interned authors, including Julie Otsuka, Yoshiko Uchida, and Brian Komei Dempster.

ii

Topaz Internment Camp was one of dozens of centers of forced incarceration established throughout the United States, in mostly remote sites. Approximately 120,000 Japanese Americans were forced to relocate to these sites in 1942 after the attack on Pearl Harbor, and many were held until 1946. The ruins left at the 640-acre Topaz site are partially visible today, with foundations for the barracks and public halls left in place, though the uninsulated modular buildings have all been relocated or sold.

iii

Shou sugi ban is a traditional method of preserving and finishing wood originating in eighteenth-century Japan. Cedar is traditionally used, and the material is charred with a torch, then sometimes wire-brushed, and an oil finish is applied. This process increases durability and makes the wood fire-retardant and resistant to insects and decay.

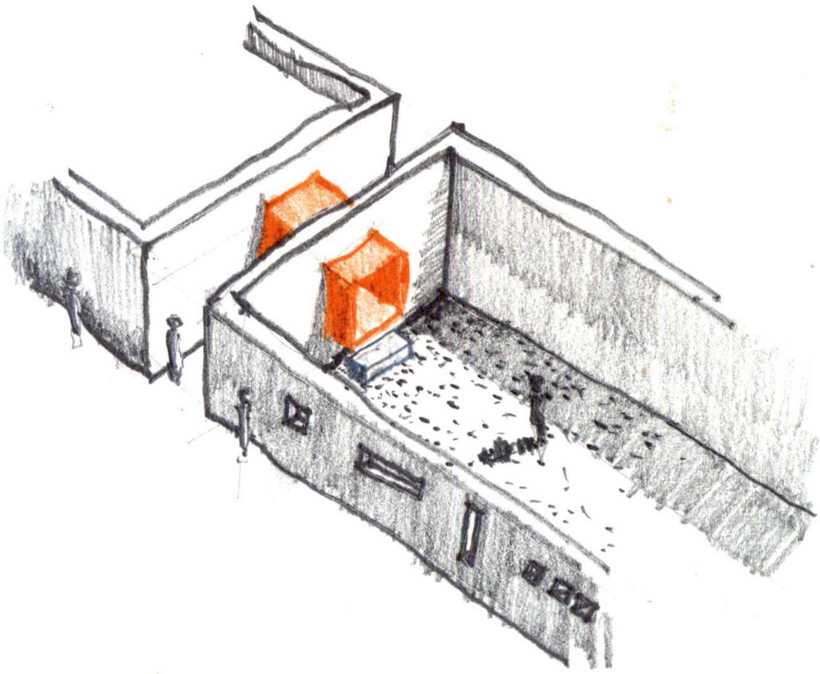

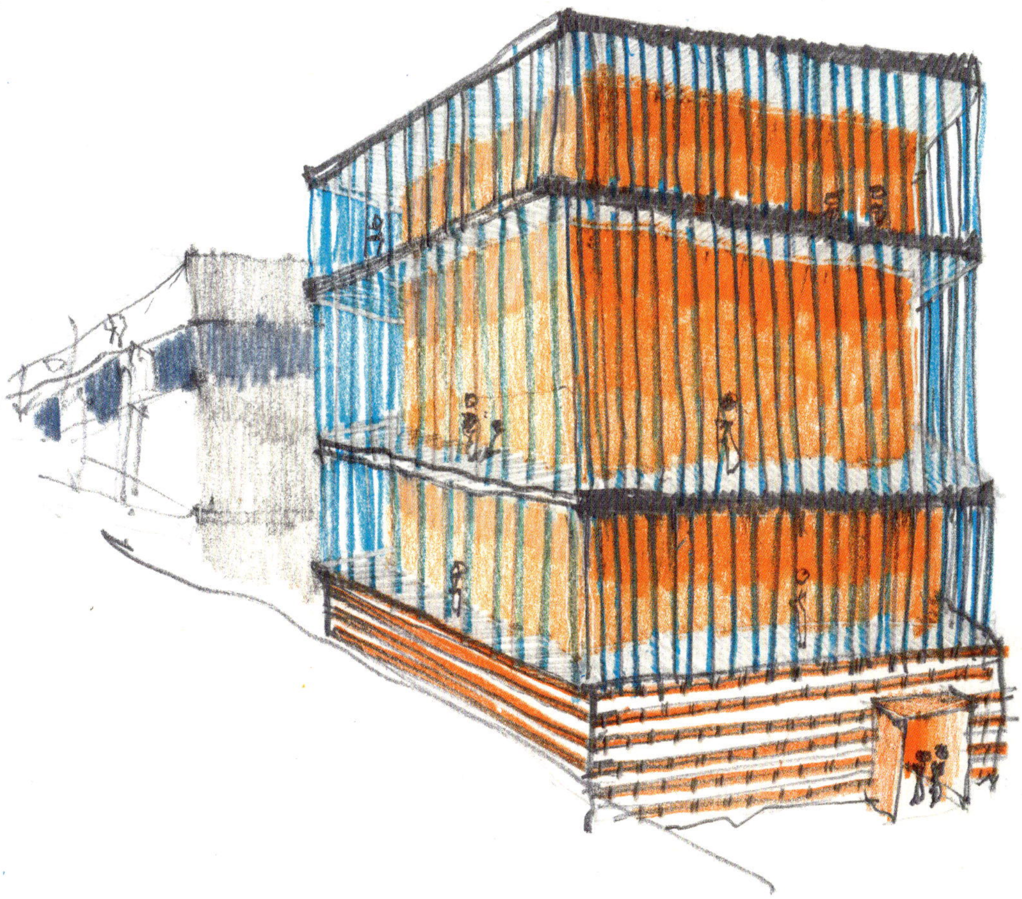

55

Topaz Museum

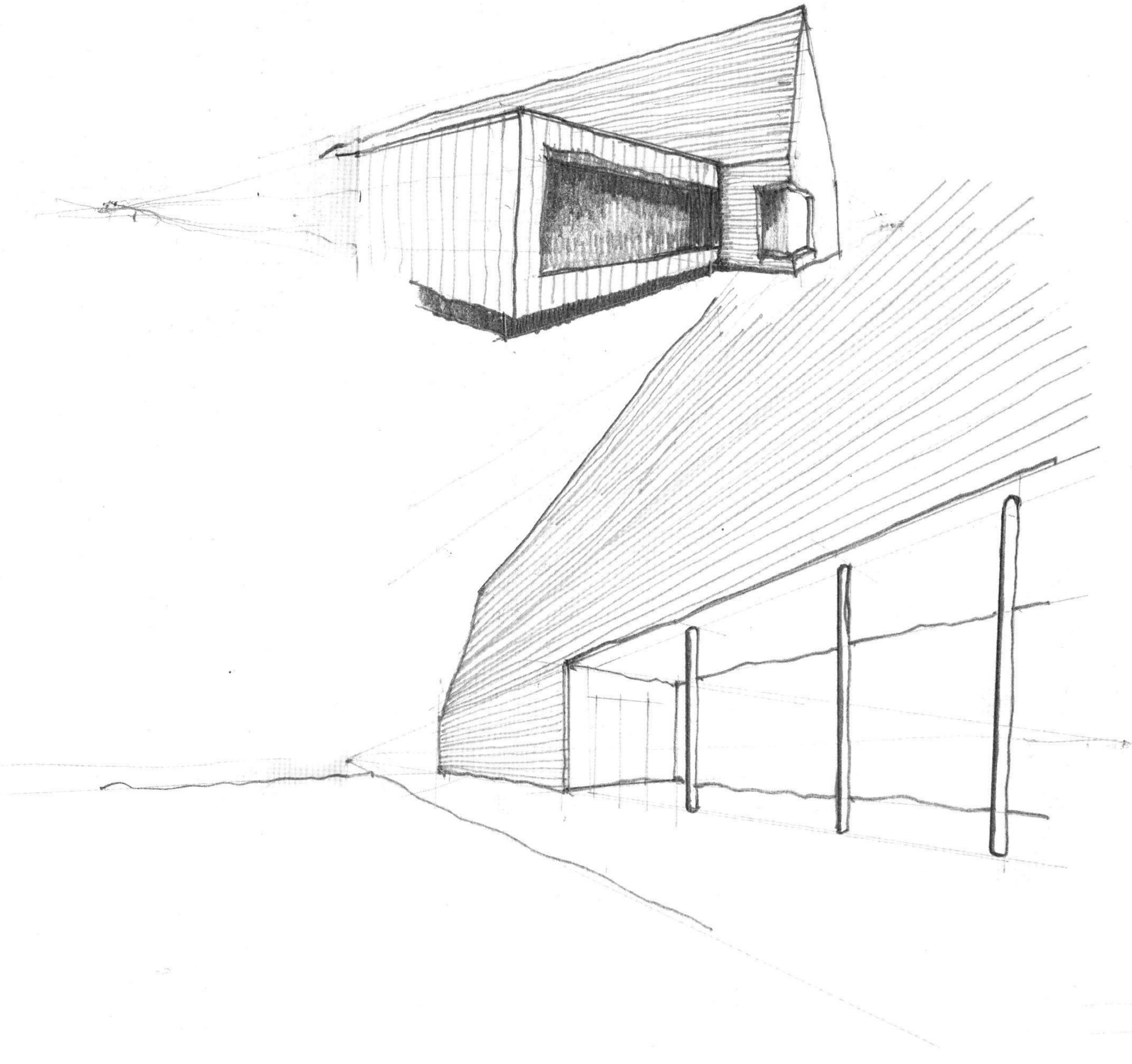

TOPAZ MUSEUM

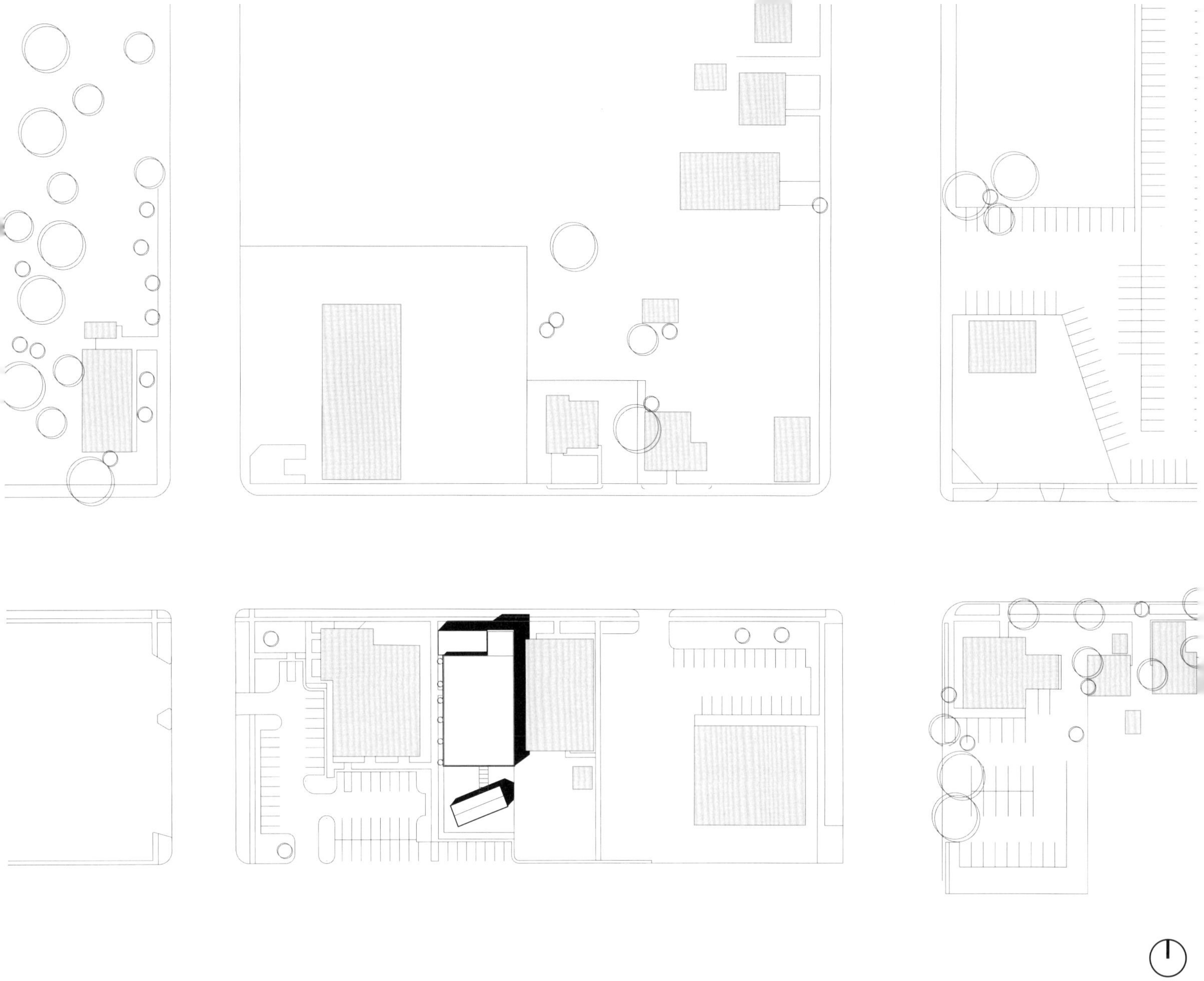

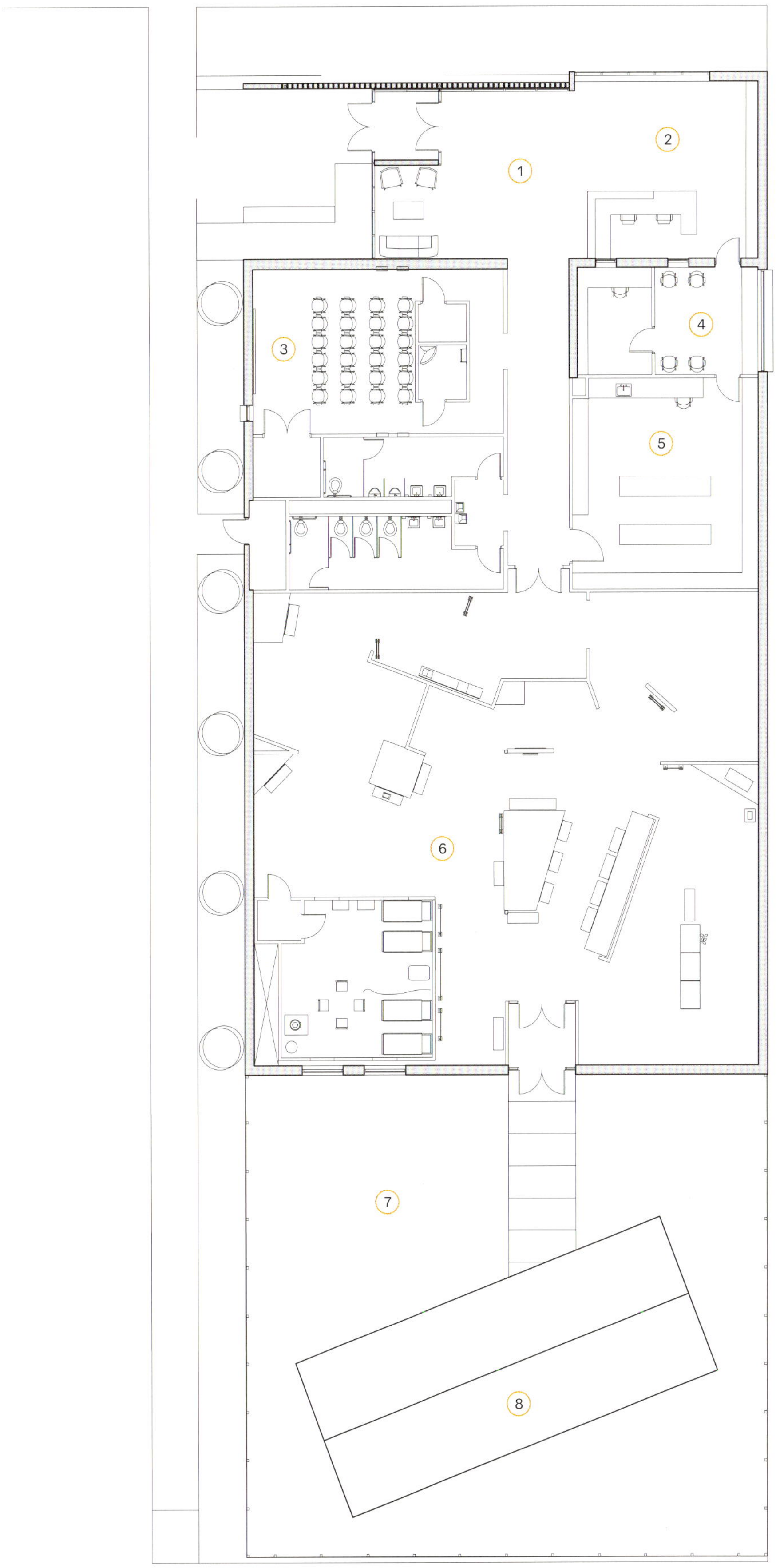

1 Lobby - Reception
2 Gift Shop
3 Education - Conference
4 Office Area
5 Curatorial Storage
6 Exhibit Space
7 Courtyard
8 Relocated Historic Recreation Hall

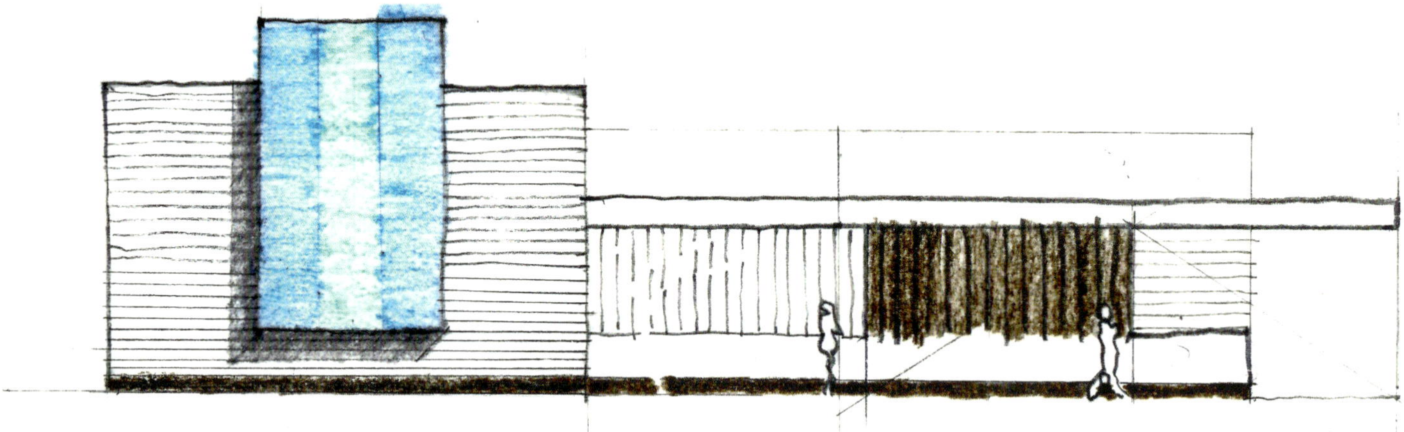

Image Captions		
	1	Museum reception area; © Brian Buroker
	2	Concept sketches; John Sparano
	3	Concept sketch; John Sparano
	4	Street view; © Brian Buroker
	5	Massing and plan study sketches; John Sparano
	6	Massing study sketches; John Sparano
	7	Main entry; © Brian Buroker
	8	Site plan
	9	Floor plan
	10	Street elevation study sketches; John Sparano

Completed	2014
Size	8,000 SF (743 m^2)
Location	Delta, Utah
Owner	Topaz Museum Board
Team	Anne Mooney Seth Striefel John Sparano
Collaborators	Darin Mano/RAW Design Excel Engineering (civil engineering) Structural Design Studio (structural engineering) David L. Jensen and Associates (mechanical engineering) Electrical Consulting Engineers (electrical engineering) West Office Exhibition Design (exhibit designers)
General Contractor	Westland Construction

Urban Treehouse

This home establishes an urban oasis surrounded by residential and commercial buildings along a tree-lined street. The space was envisioned as a sanctuary—simultaneously inviting and protective. The design process began with a study of sacred spaces and led to the proposal of a pure geometric volume as the home's form with light carefully brought into its interior. The architects minimized the footprint of the home while maximizing its spatial experience through the consideration of architectural scale, proportion, light, and materials.[i]

The program for the home includes spaces for a large, open-plan entertaining zone with kitchen, dining, and living areas, a primary suite, and a small pool and guesthouse. The idea of home as a respite from the world is evident through nature splicing into the form's massing in a series of courtyards. The design reconciles seemingly polar desires: to feel secluded yet open; to be connected yet separate from the outside world. This residential sanctuary feels simultaneously inviting and protective within the context of urban life, incorporating a series of indoor-outdoor spaces—from a front porch facing the street to a secluded outdoor backyard bathing retreat.

The home incorporates spaces for entertaining guests, both indoors and out, and private retreat spaces, including a meditation room, all connected to the three courtyard gardens. These public and private spaces open out to embrace the urban site in which the house is securely nestled. The public facade opens to a front porch with hardscape that doubles as a parking area. Blackened cedarwood skins the envelope, and a green-gray concrete floor surface flows from the exterior deck through the interior spaces. The massing establishes a strong connection to the outdoors and the city, while the plan emphasizes a flowing, connected, open space for the owner to live and work.

A double-height, covered front porch entry and facade are created with full-height glazing. Inside, the home wraps around a central courtyard with a pool accessible from both the great room and guesthouse. This space forms an outdoor gathering area for residents and guests alike. A bridge connects the public space and primary suite located above the pool house, which is serenely private with a clerestory of east-facing windows bringing abundant morning light into the suite.

The pool is located in the central courtyard and connects the great room on the west to the guesthouse on the east through full-height sliding glass doors. With open doors, the public spaces, pool, and guesthouse become one continuous indoor/outdoor space. By placing the swimming pool at the center of the site, the courtyard becomes a gathering point for entertaining and is protected from the street frontage and a busy commercial lot behind the property. Powder and utility rooms are located on the northern side, concealed by an open stairway and bridge to the primary suite.

The Urban Treehouse brings a sense of peace and renewal to the neighborhood. The effect is a home perceived from the street as inviting and accessible. The massing establishes a strong connection to the street, to its history and urban context, and to nature. The plan emphasizes flowing, connected, open spaces, while simultaneously providing the comforting respite of a sanctuary.

i
The proportions of the architecture, including the front elevation, were influenced by the golden section. Sparano + Mooney Architecture has employed sacred proportional geometries in this and other projects, and referenced the work of György Doczi, and his book *The Power of Limits: Proportional Harmonies in Nature, Art, and Architecture*, in developing the elevations and spaces.

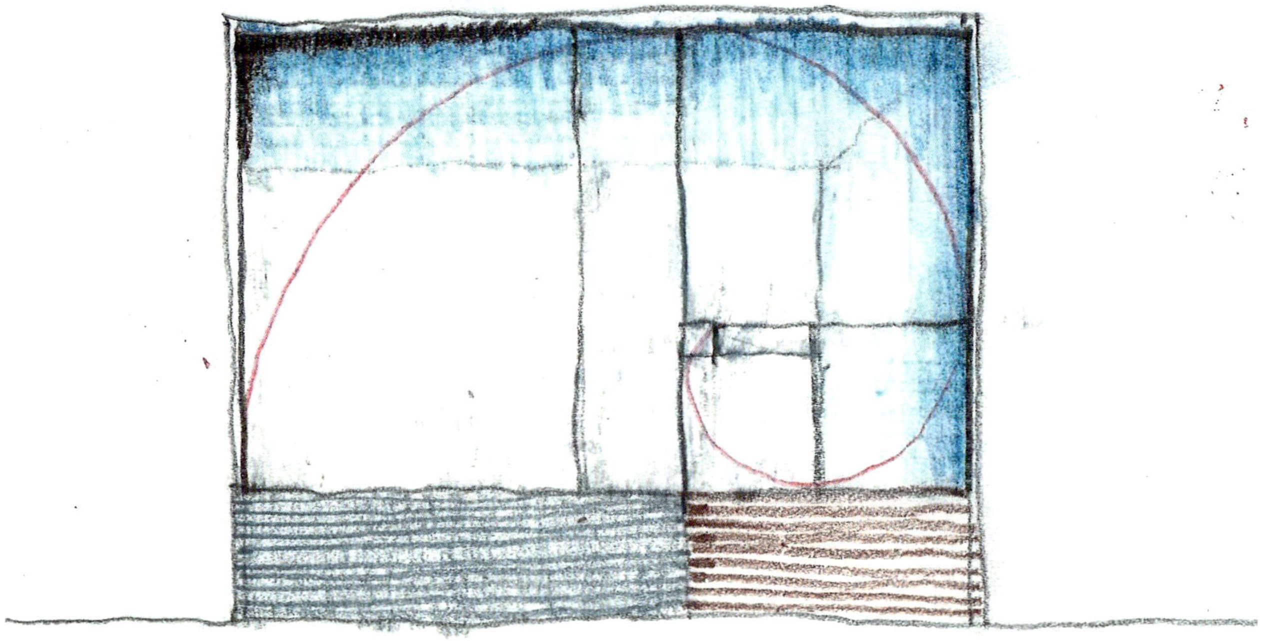

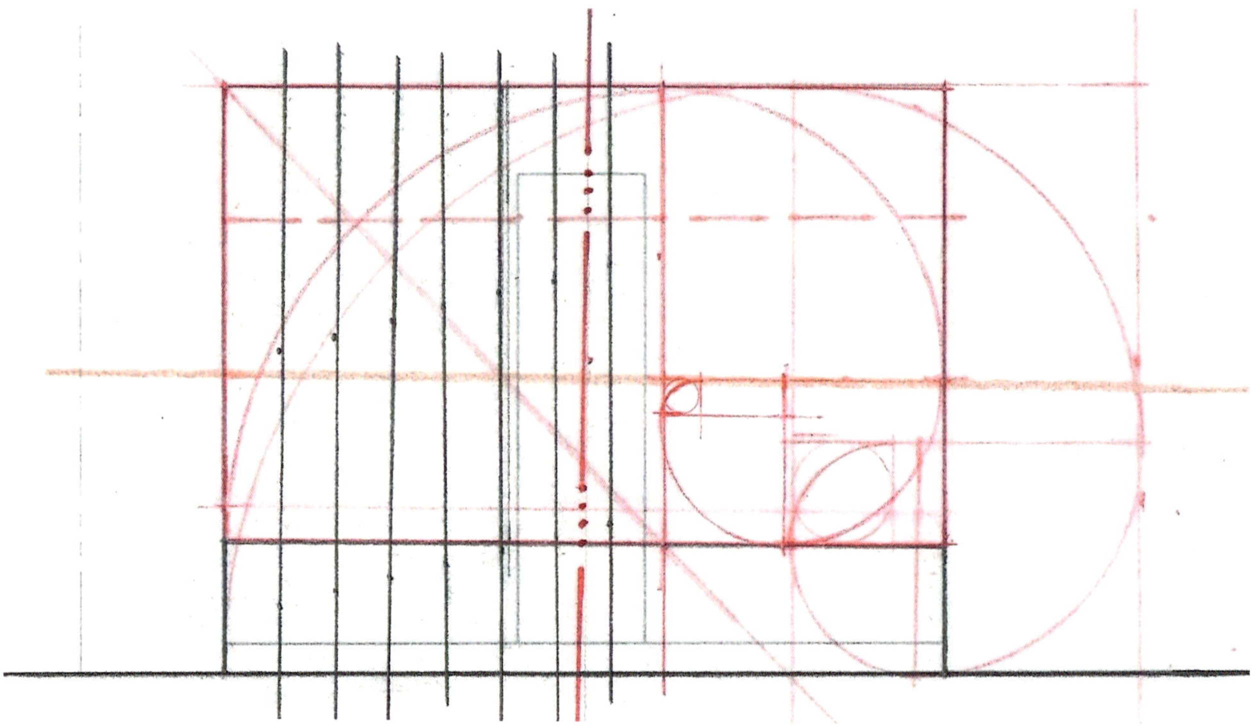

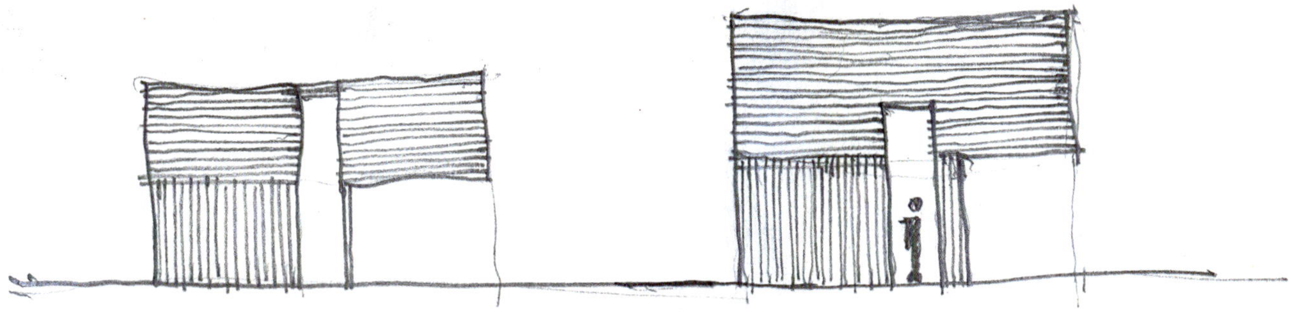

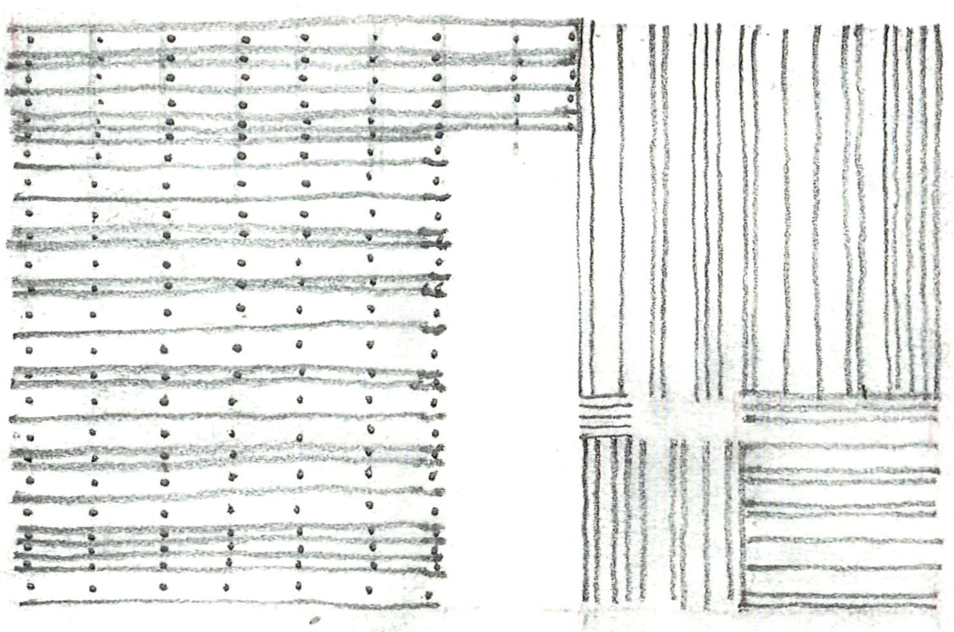

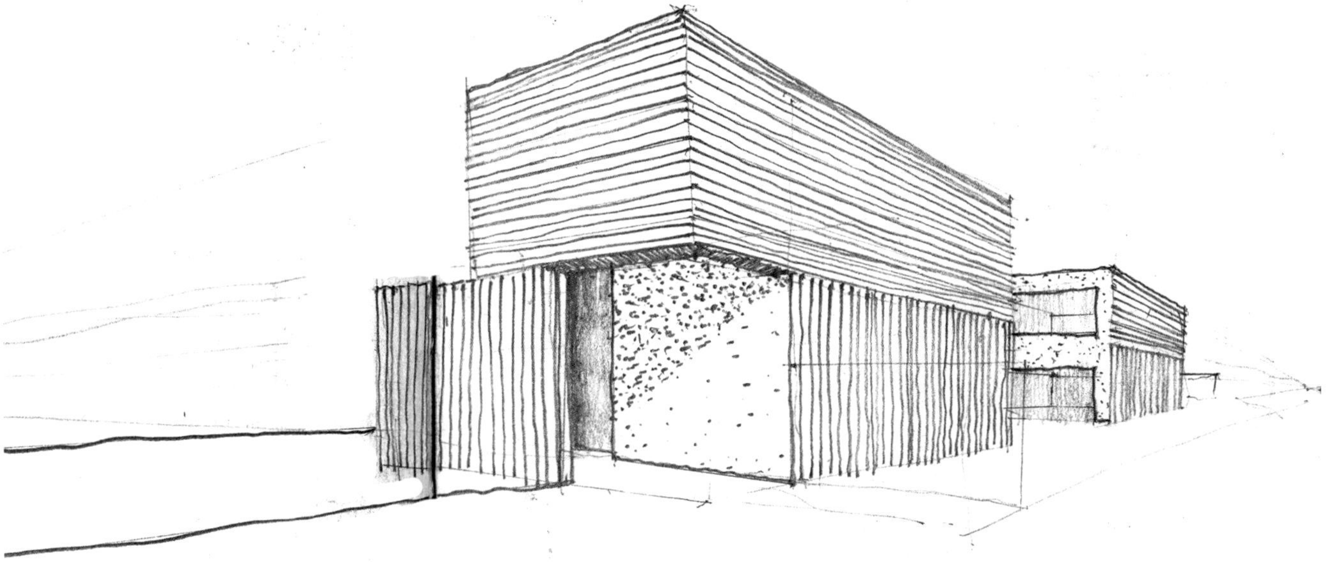

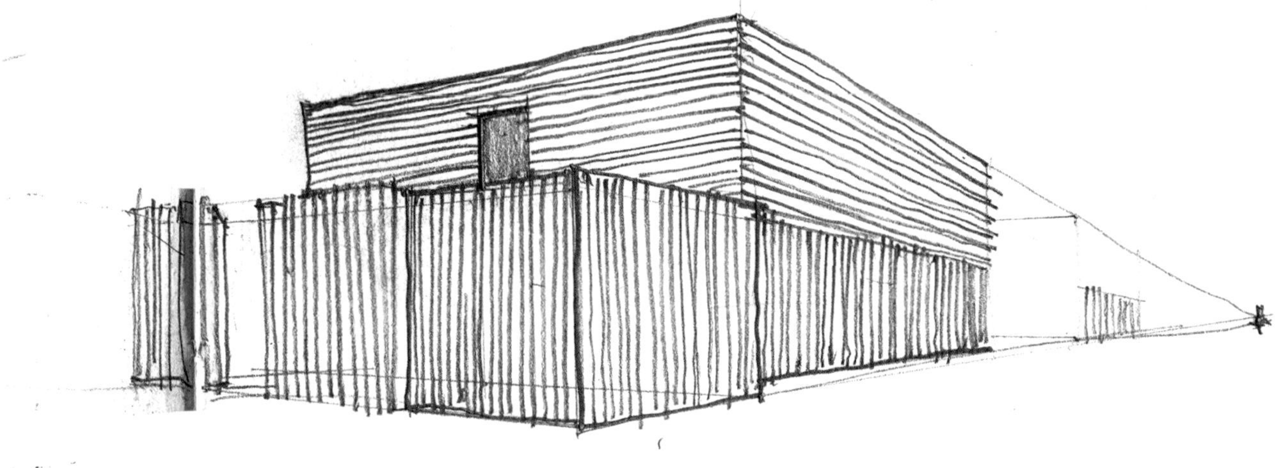

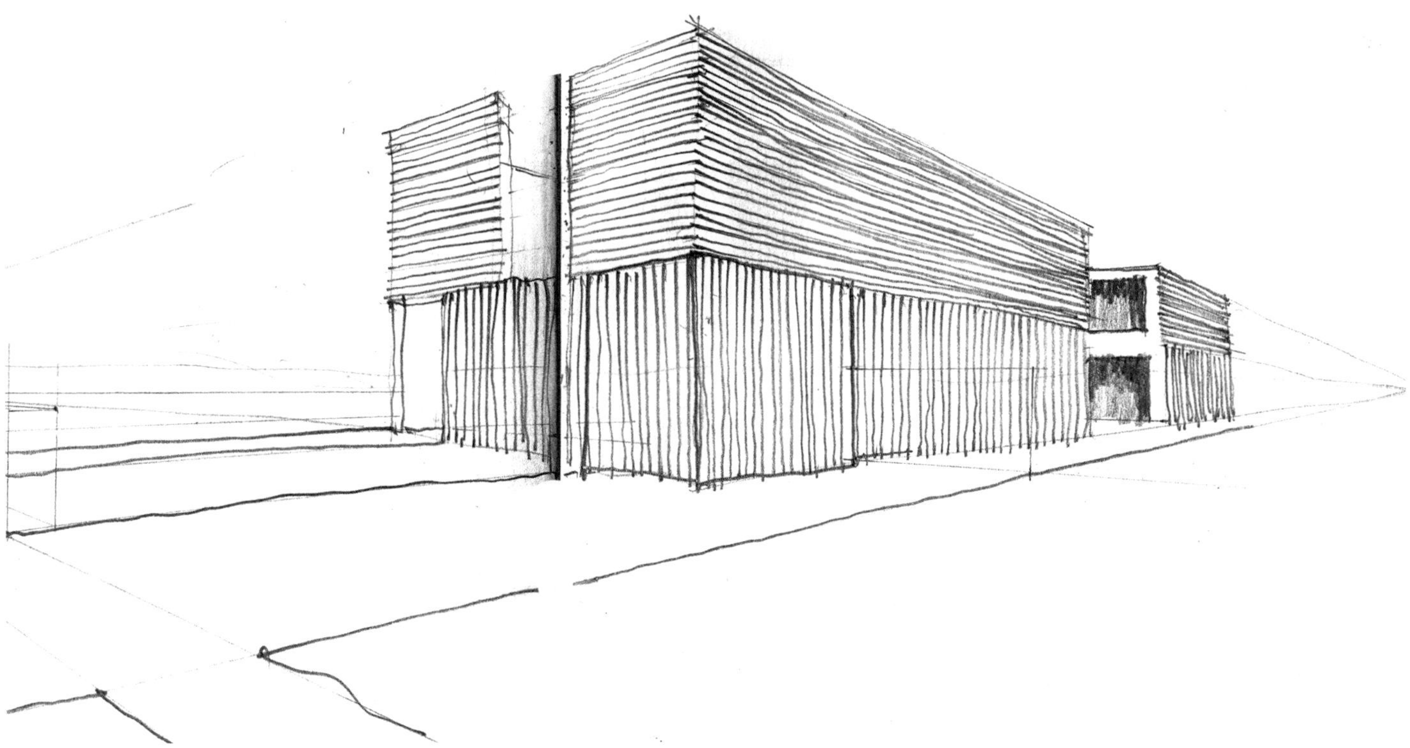

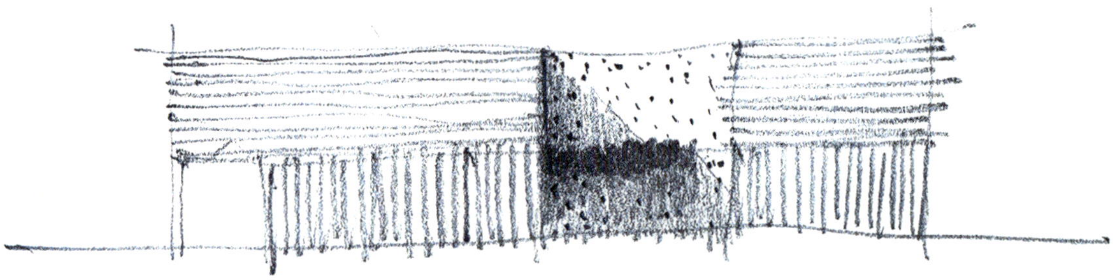

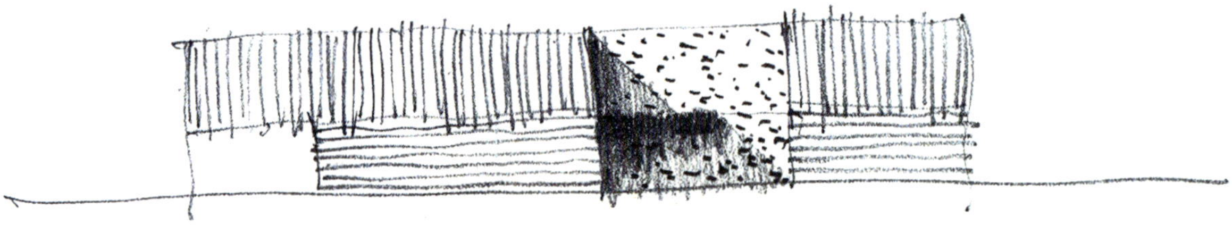

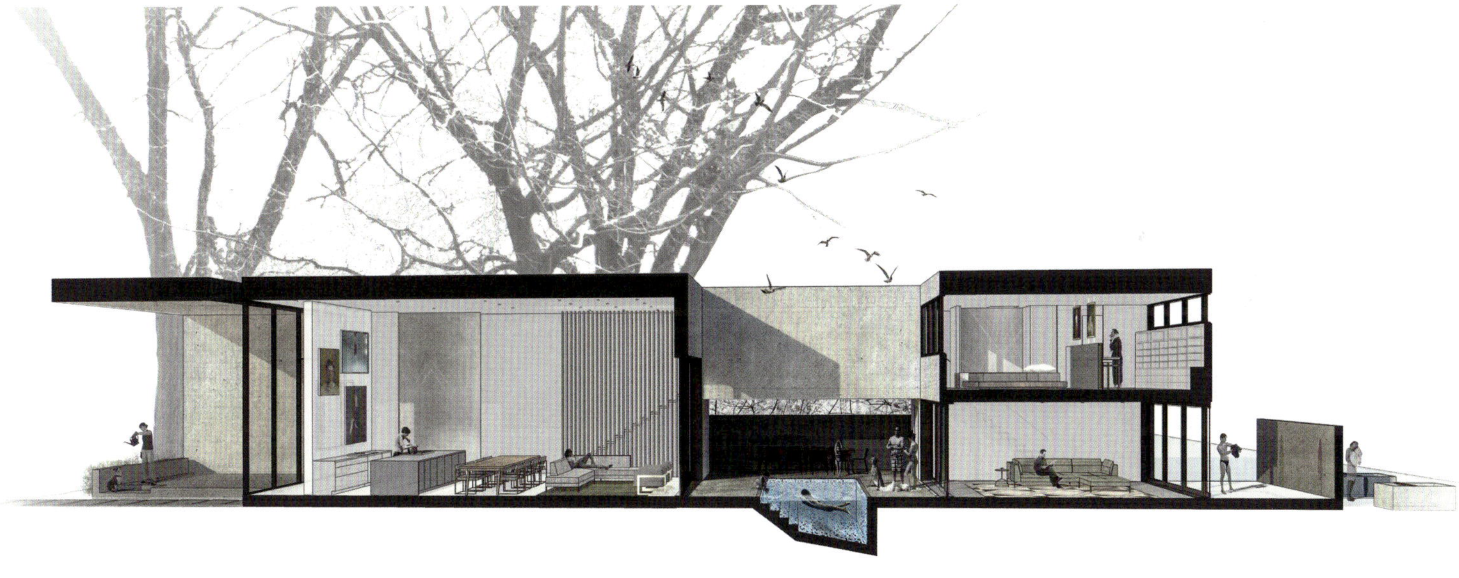

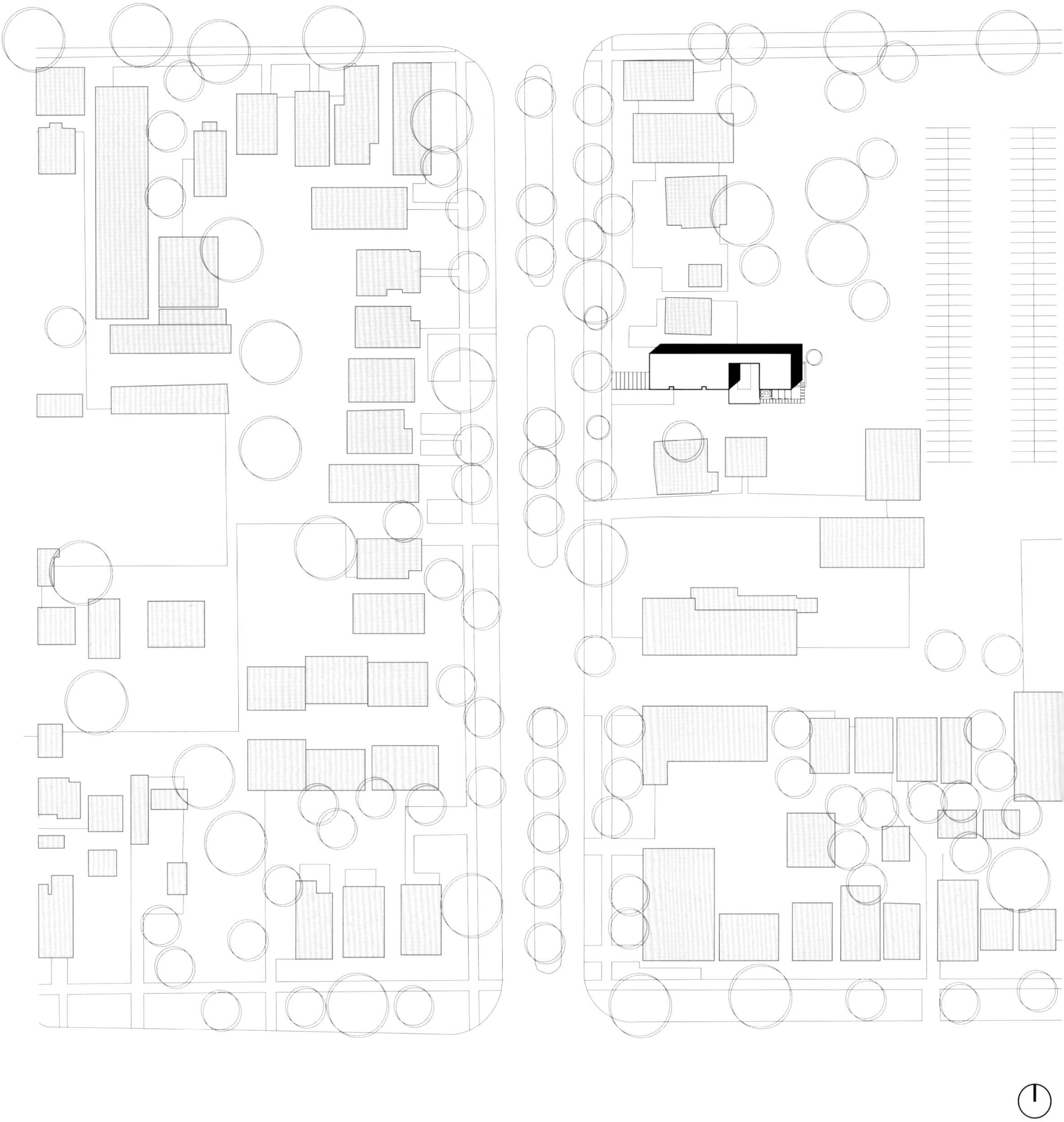

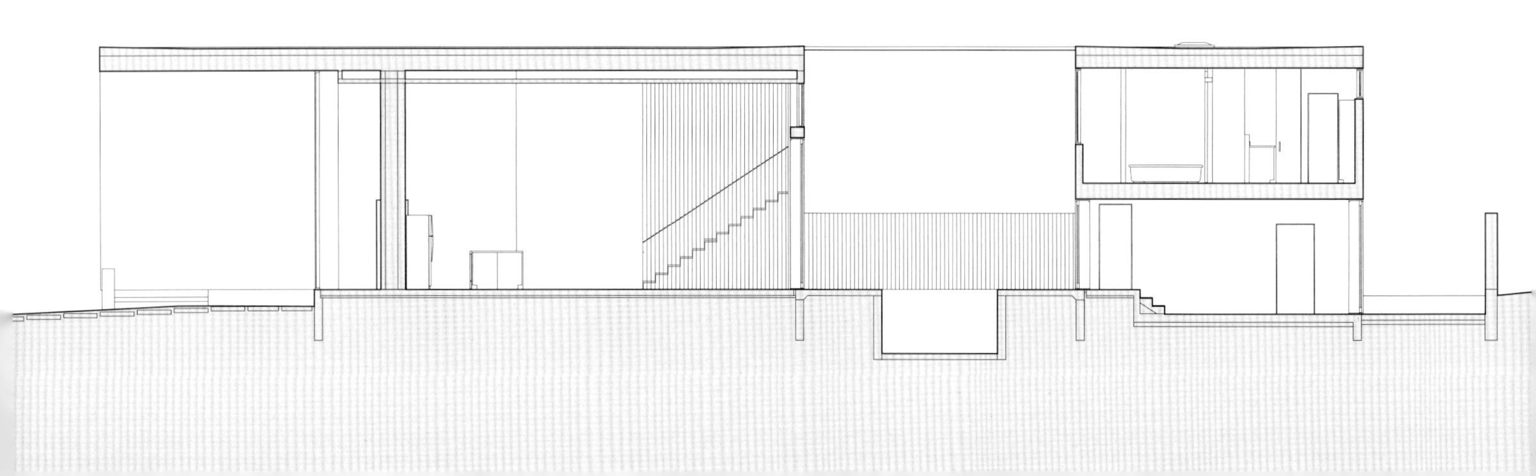

Image Captions

1 Entrance looking toward street; © Matt Winquist
2 Concept model
3 Concept model
4 Street facade study sketches; John Sparano
5 Street facade study sketches; John Sparano
6 Primary facade / entrance; © Matt Winquist
7 Massing studies; John Sparano
8 View of entrance; © Matt Winquist
9 Final model (detail)
10 Side view of entrance; © Matt Winquist
11 Final model
South elevation studies; John Sparano
12 East elevation (detail); © Matt Winquist
Final model base (detail)
13 Front porch; © Matt Winquist
14 Perspective rendering
Rendered cross-section
15 Site plan
Building section
16 Final model
17 Courtyard view; © Kerri Fukui
18 View into great room; © Matt Winquist
19 View of street facade; © Matt Winquist

Completed	2019
Size	2,100 SF (195 m²)
Location	Salt Lake City, Utah
Team	John Sparano Anne Mooney Seth Striefel Nate King Philip Dimick Jun Li David Kirk (model)
Collaborators	Structural Design Studio (structural engineering) City Home Collective (interior design): Cody Derrick, Lauren Bald, Rebecca Loosli
General Contractor	Sausage

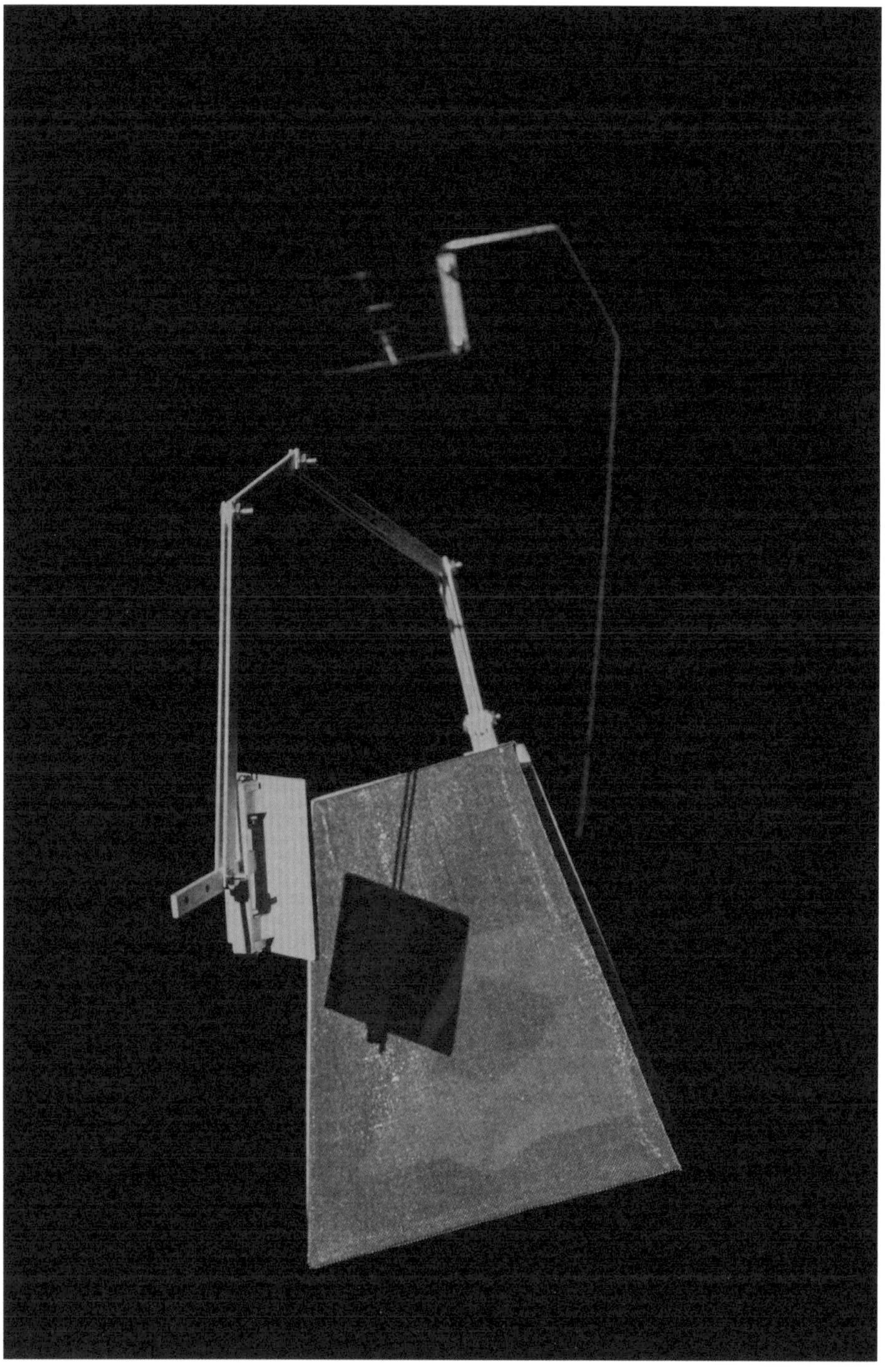

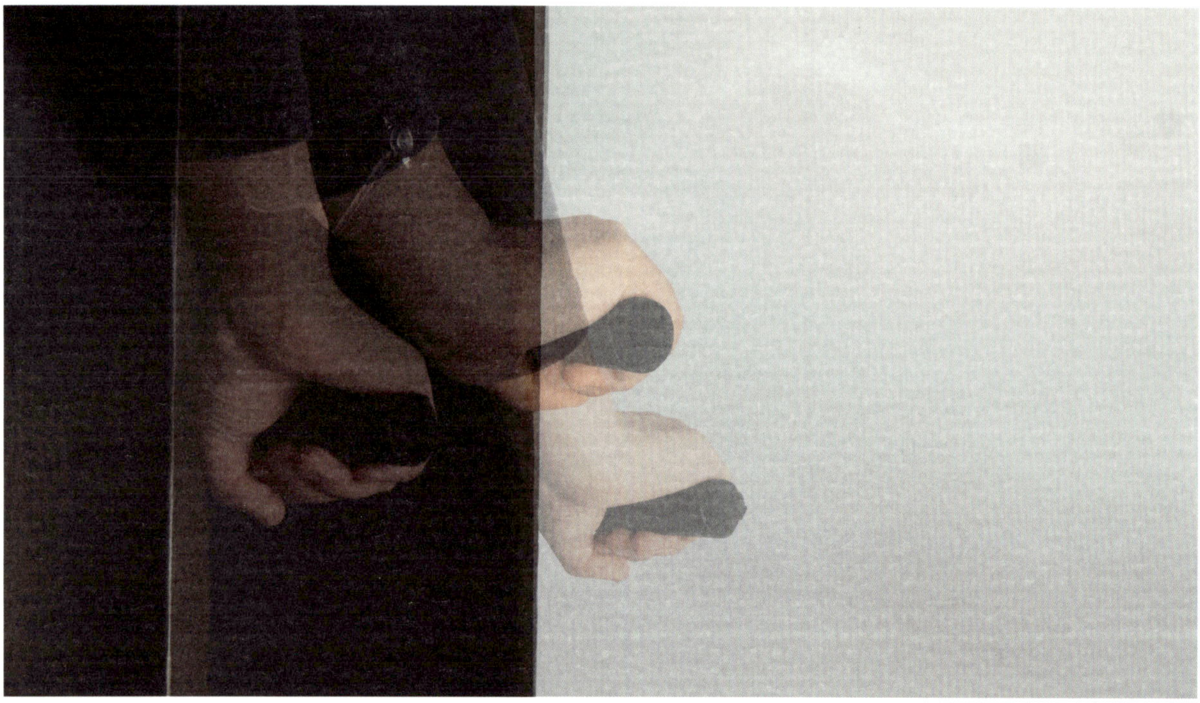

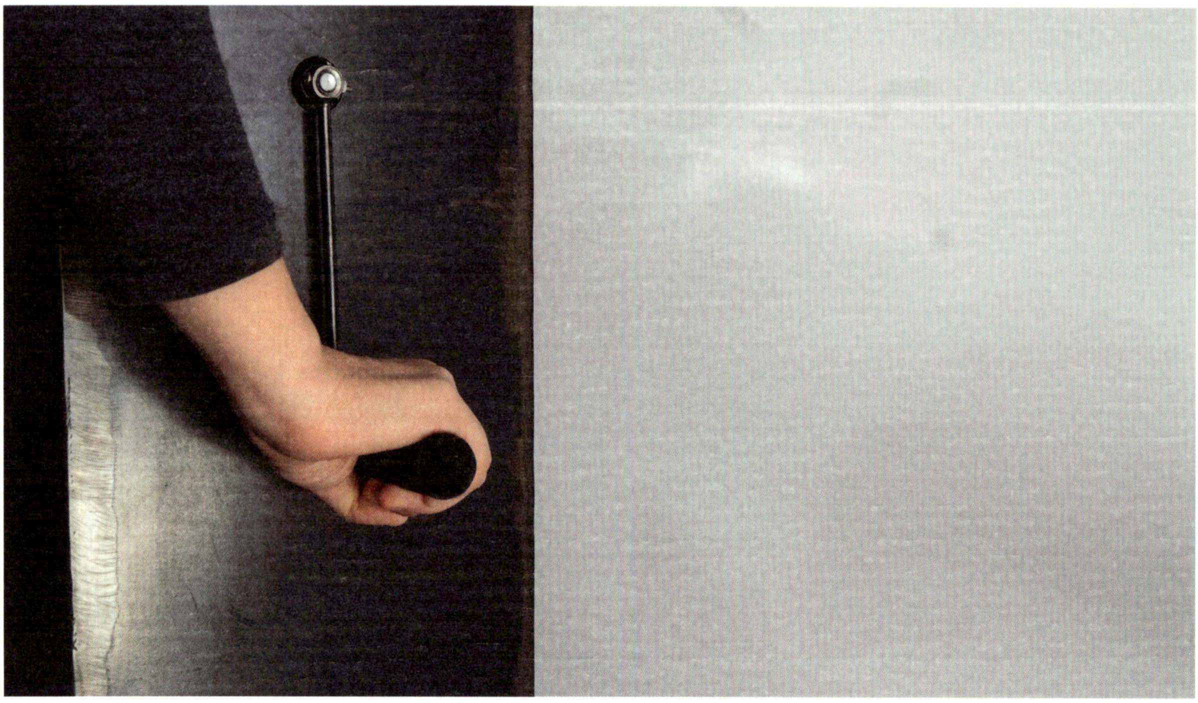

REALITY ONLY
REVEALS ITSELF
WHEN IT IS
ILLUMINATED
BY A RAY OF
POETRY
George Braque

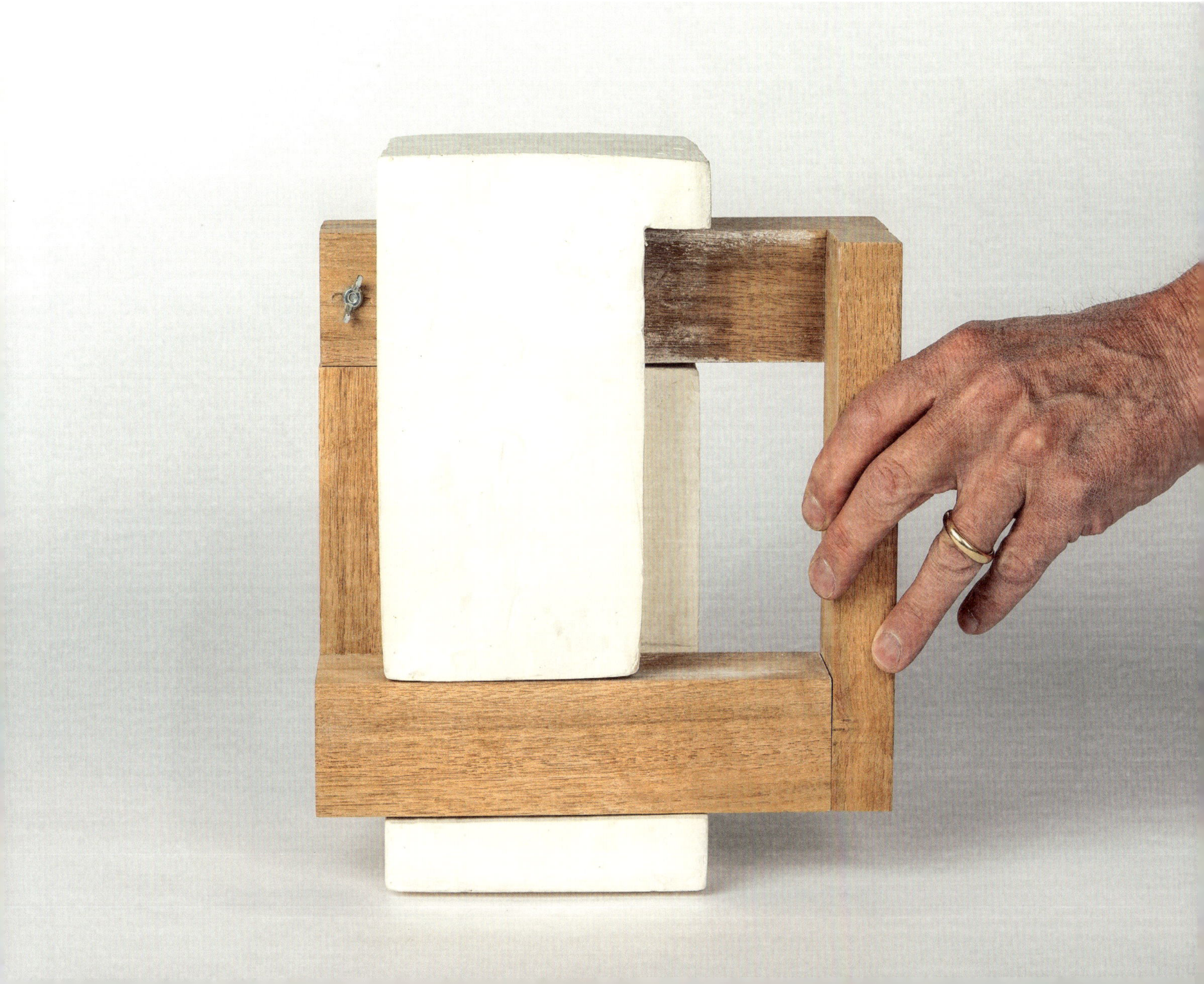

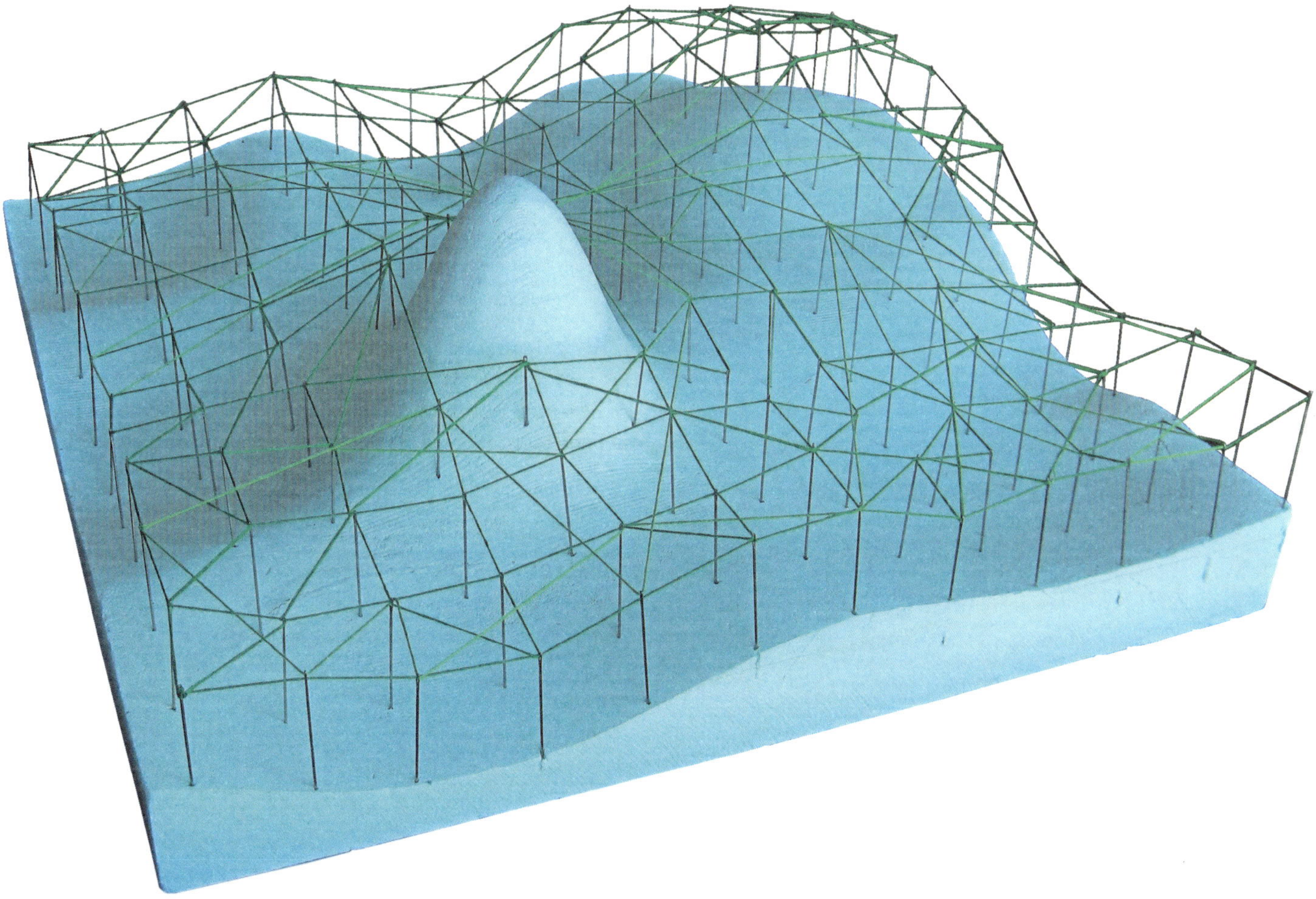

Image Captions

1 Glashausen
2 Port-au-Prince Cathedral
3 Urban Treehouse
4 Urban Treehouse
5 Urban Treehouse (detail)
6 Urban Treehouse
7 Urban Treehouse (detail)
8 Gilb Museum of Arcadia Heritage
9 Gilb Museum of Arcadia Heritage
10 Buddhist Hermitage
11 Buddhist Hermitage
12 Nora Eccles Harrison Museum of Art
13 Nora Eccles Harrison Museum of Art
14 Aurora Villa
15 Aurora Villa
16 Wabi-Sabi
17 Wabi-Sabi
18 Preserve Residence
19 Kimball Art Center
20 Park City Residence
21 Park City Residence
22 Emigration Canyon Residence (detail)
23 Emigration Canyon Residence
24 Pulsar Residence

John Sparano

THE
H E U R I S T I C
PROCESS

heuristic [hyoo-ris-tik or, often, yoo-]

i to learn, discover, understand, or solve problems by experimenting with or evaluating possible solutions by trial and error.
ii of, relating to, or based on experimentation, evaluation, or trial-and-error methods.
iii serving to indicate or point out; stimulating interest as a means of furthering investigation.

process [pros-es; especially British proh-ses]

i a systematic series of actions directed to some end.
ii a continuous action, operation, or series of changes taking place in a definite manner.

device [dih-vahys]

i a thing made for a particular purpose; an invention or contrivance, especially a mechanical or electrical one.

Random House Webster's Unabridged Dictionary, 2nd ed., s.v.

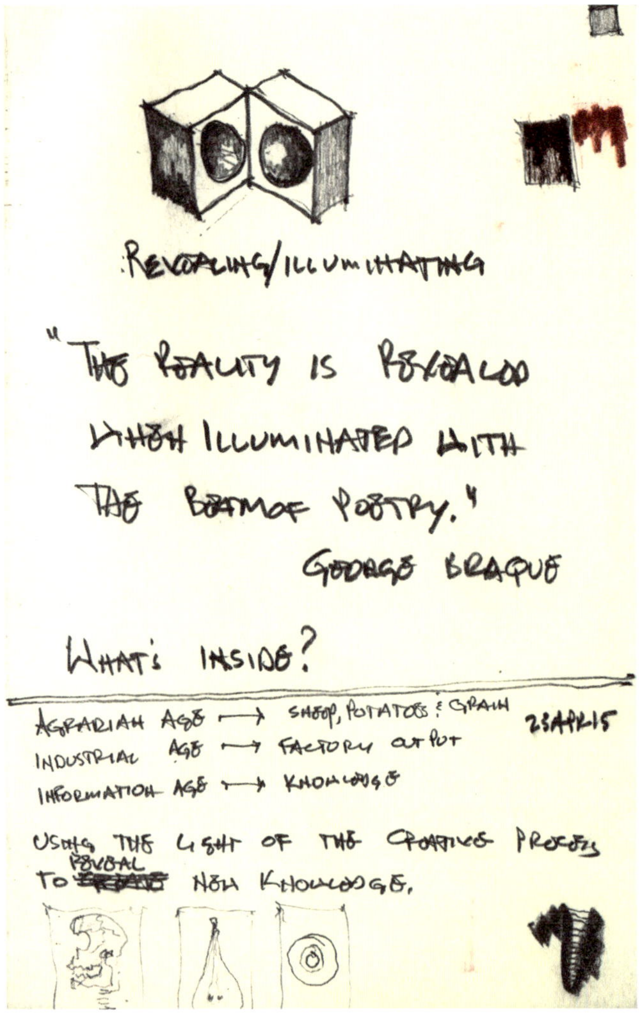

Early writing and sketching in search of NEHMA design concept, 2015

The presence of an idea constitutes the difference between a building and architecture. Our belief in this is not so different from how many architects see the distinction between architecture and construction. The idea gives us something to aim at, a target, a means by which we evaluate the relative success or failure of any proposed architecture. Without this idea, we have no basis for determining right from wrong, good from bad. Without it, the process is lost; architecture cannot exist.

What is different is the process we have developed to identify, evolve, and apply an idea to built form and space. If we effectively employ this process, the project team is equipped to fully comprehend what leads to a successful architectural solution. Clearly delineating the means by which design choices will be made facilitates robust architectural discourse in the studio. If the parameters by which a proposed solution will be judged are available to all, the entire team has the means and ability to contribute thoughtfully to the evolution of the architecture.

The power to evaluate a proposed architectural gesture is no longer the sole province of a studio head. Because our value system for the decision-making process is not intuitive nor administered at the discretion of a "master architect" figure, anyone—from the most junior intern to a partner—can propose ideas for consideration when the process is democratized in this way. Understanding and engaging in this design process allows us to more fully engage the latent potential within each set of project conditions.

Our process also affords a method for being vigilant in avoiding clichés and fashion as we work. It leads us toward considering more idiosyncratic solutions

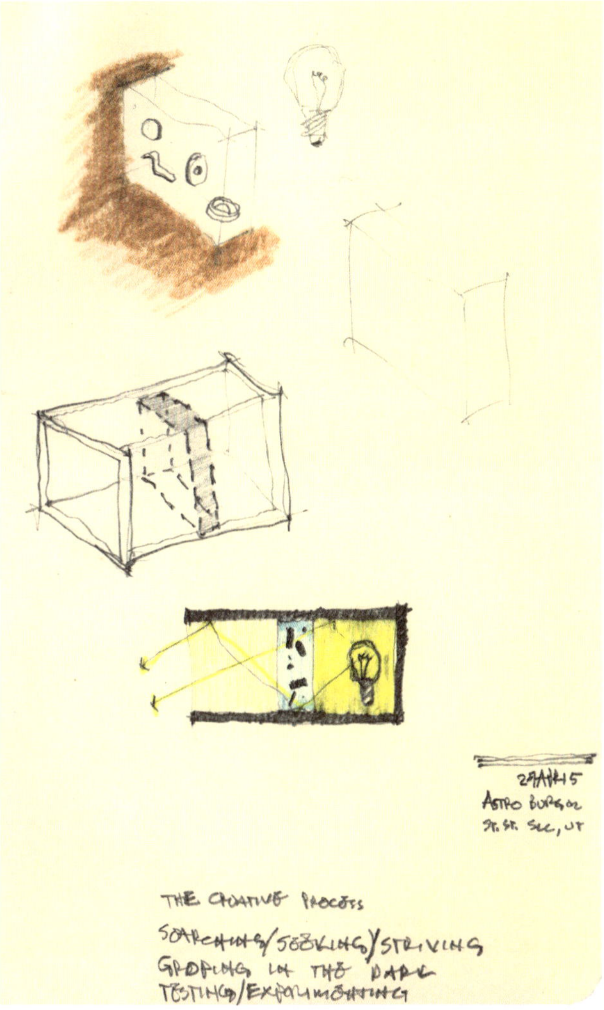

Development sketches for NEHMA heuristic device, 2015

that spring from unexpected origins. It focuses our processes on uncovering formal and spatial configurations in relation to the core idea established for the project, allowing us to avoid architectural gestures appropriated directly from the architectural press and their unrelated associations and meanings.

This way of working provides a means of moving beyond our preconceptions. By examining every project's relationship to its conceptual framework, we force ourselves to consider each constituent part thoroughly. Invention is implicit and our way of ensuring we don't backslide into the use of typical details or familiar outcomes. Having said that, if a traditional solution is agreed to be the one that best responds to the idea, it is pursued with intention.

To describe our process, our approach to the architectural impulse, and how we propose to transcend mere building and move closer to architecture, we begin with the conditions of site, program, client, and context. Ideas are found within these given conditions, with the most compelling concept drafted into service as the genesis of the project.

Through rigorous investigation, we reach an irreducible core, which forms the idea. This exploration may begin with something seemingly insignificant, but as we investigate, our preconceptions fall away, and we see it anew as something with profound value. And from that infinitely tiny seed, we begin the design process.

The critical task at this point is to choose exactly which idea will go forward. The research functions of the practice lead us to this choice. Sometimes a singular text or line of investigation inspires the idea; other times, a concept is addressed and expanded upon through multiple sources.

Final NEHMA heuristic device, 2015

To develop the idea, we explore its permutations, tangents, and variations, and gradually come to know it more fully. Every concept is composed of multiple closely-related or tangential ideas. We are interested in the core. What is it about this concept that links it most strongly to the idiosyncrasies of the project? What is the essence of it? What cannot be stripped away without sacrificing clarity?

Once we've amassed a body of knowledge, we synthesize and interrogate it through writing. The writing, once it becomes insufficient in expressing the direction of the work, gradually tapers into sketching. These very early sketches are the first attempts at grappling with how to speak to a core idea using something other than words. Sketches, drawings, and three-dimensional constructs all might embody this thinking. We've come to describe these objects as "heuristic devices."

The heuristic device is not a scale model of a building. It is not representational. There is typically no formal or visual connection between this construct and the completed structure. The shared link is the idea, manifest in different mediums—sculpture and architecture. We intend no visual connection between the conceptual model and the architecture, but the idea must exist in both.

The conceptual construct serves as a repository of the idea identified as the progenitor of the project. The connection between idea and architecture makes it critical that the device is fabricated and honed to reinforce the concept as strongly as possible. This singular point of contact between the two functions is not unlike a membrane—woven of translation and filtering out clichés, fashion, and preconceptions. Only the idea should pass through this filter moving from conceptual construct toward architecture.

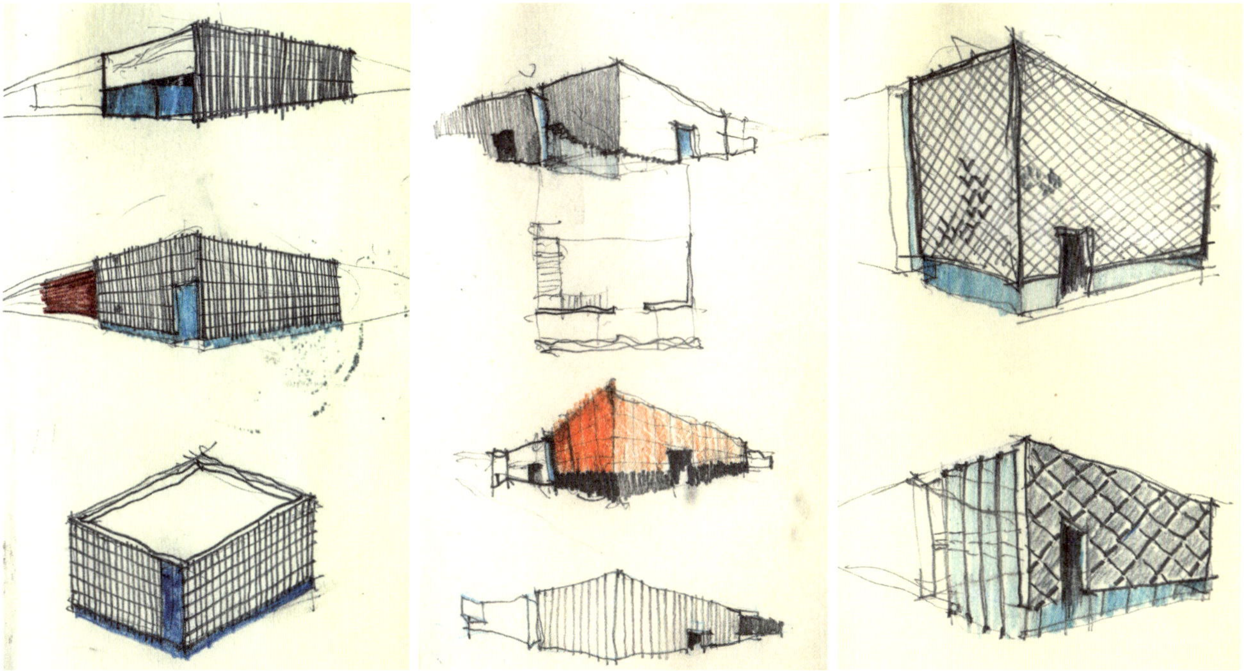

Architectural development sketches for NEHMA, 2016

The process of creating a heuristic device is the quest to conceive a construct that embodies an idea. We seek to arrive at a physical object that speaks fully and succinctly to the research we have conducted. This phase, too, begins with thinking things through on the pages of our sketchbooks. It is a process of casting about until we find the most articulate translation into form. We search for an assembly of materials that most closely brushes up against the central idea.

Sketching becomes sketching objects, building mock-ups, and constructing final heuristic devices. The detail and craft of the device are meaningful because we depend on these objects to capture and embody the essence of the research. Testing material combinations and evaluating the appropriateness of joinery options are why the study models are invaluable to the success of each construct. The construction of the device is based on its relationship to the core project idea. An exposed fastener conveys a different meaning than a concealed connection of materials, as details embody significance when translated into architectural expression. Which one is more consistent with the idea? The final object is the sum of those decisions. It is what we sit on the table in our design meetings to remind ourselves of the project's conceptual underpinnings and our common understanding of what the eventual architectural proposal must reflect.

This process provides us with a conceptual foundation for answering the question, why? Why did we organize the program elements in the way we did? Why is its massing horizontal and not vertical? Why does it sit so lightly or imbed itself within the site? Why is it clad in that material?, etc. While this process is not absolutely objective, the heuristic process and resultant device provide common ground for understanding the project origin and, if we accept it, a basis to evaluate potential architectural solutions. Without a conceptual framework, there is only intuition, personal preference, and the capricious subjectivity of opinion. The discourse remains within the realm of the subjective.

The final step, the most difficult one—the translation from abstract studies into architecture—also begins with freehand sketching and analog exploration. Because the process is now informing the function of a built structure, dimensionality and

Architectural model iterations for NEHMA, 2016

scale are also relevant. Here, the evolution of the design moves into the digital realm, both two-dimensionally and three-dimensionally. Digital or analog, the goal is the same: to generate design options for large or small aspects of the architecture that can be tested against a central idea.

The foundational idea makes its way into the architecture through the continuous testing and evaluation of design scenarios. In this way, trial and error become the primary means of finding the most significant architectural solutions. Each incremental iteration of the architecture is held up for debate in the studio: How does it relate to the thinking embodied in the heuristic device? If a strong relationship is evident, that iteration remains a part of the project. If not, it fails, and we move on to something else. We try again, and we may fail again, but with each failure, we learn something. No attempt is a total failure. No increment is a complete success either, so we go on, we explore other directions, we move through what seem to be barriers or limits, beyond dead ends.

In spite of being occasionally frustrated by this process, we do not fear or avoid it. We are not afraid of missteps, because, at the very least, we have come to understand that employing this process provides us with a means to determine when we are on the right path and when we are wandering astray. It puts the circumstances in place that allow an idea to be present in our work. And with that placement, it is possible for architecture to exist.

Saint Joseph the Worker Catholic Church

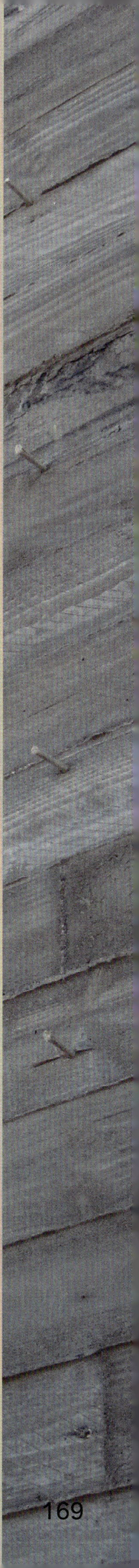

The life of Saint Joseph the Worker, known as the patron saint of laborers, inspired the architecture of this new Catholic church in West Jordan, Utah. The design process began with research into the life of Saint Joseph and a parallel exploration of the history of this faith community. Saint Joseph, often depicted with tools, was a carpenter and, like many of the parishioners, worked with his hands. Working-class immigrants came to this part of the American West for employment in the mines or on the railroad and often remained in the area.[i] The original church, outdated and slated for demolition, was built by these tradespeople and funded by small donations made by the faithful to erect the modest structure. The design of the new church reuses fundamental elements of the old building and incorporates new steel, copper, and hand-crafted wood components referencing the parish's mining and construction history. This approach made visible the project's social and cultural lineage, and contributed to its environmental sustainability.

The architecture emerged as a collective set of programmed niches within a thickened oval form. These dense walls created the sanctuary space and support the roof. Thickened walls have a rich historical precedent in sacred architecture, and in following this lineage, the architecture of Saint Joseph the Worker contains small chapels and statuary and storage areas within the perimeter shell.[ii] Light is brought in through a sandblasted glazed band forming the base of the building. This base is capped by a thick, textural concrete volume punctuated by colored glass openings. The architecture of the main sanctuary is organized by two offset ellipses. The space between these ellipses, the *poché* space, creates a zone for liturgical functions, including a chapel, a reconciliation room, prayer niches, and areas for statuary and religious art. The elliptical form of the church was conceived of as an ideal gathering geometry without corners, facilitating active participation by the community.

The upper portion of the ellipse contains windows that relate in form, scale, and color to research conducted on the lives of the twelve apostles. These windows feature glazed colored panels, an abstracted expression of, and affordable alternative to, traditional stained glass. The day chapel, used for daily worship, is clad with copper panels donated from a local mining company.[iii] The chapel's interior is an expression of a singular material—tongue and groove vertical grain fir—from wall base to roof, all illuminated by a single, clear skylight.

The material palette for the church consists of common elements that parishioners confront in their everyday lives: concrete, wood, metal, and glass. The design incorporates these familiar materials, manipulated and detailed to become extraordinary. As they are transformed by the "worker," they are crafted into surfaces expressing the skill of a tradesperson rather than the unfinished qualities of the raw material. The modest, humble nature of these ordinary materials configured within new architectural forms and surfaces seeks to both reassure and inspire, with the highly textured, board-formed concrete mass and handcrafted wood elements forming the altar backdrop, ceiling, and pews. Copper is reserved for the most sacred aspects of the church, cladding the skylight over the altar and the exterior of the day chapel. The use of copper also reminds the community of its mining roots and parish history.

i

People from Ireland, Italy, China, Japan, and Greece migrated to Utah and the surrounding states in the nineteenth century to work in copper, silver, and coal mines, and as laborers on the construction of the transcontinental railroad. Some of the early parishioners of Saint Joseph the Worker were miners living in a company town on the outskirts of Kennecott Copper Mine. When expansion of the mine forced workers out of their homes, many moved to what is now the city of West Jordan, and the early parish was formed.

ii

During the design process, the architects drew from Christian architectural precedents, including Borromini's San Carlo alle Quattro Fontane church and Bramante's Tempietto chapel. These examples of Renaissance and Baroque Roman architecture consist of masonry structures and contain occupiable perimeter walls. The spaces within the *poché* have a historic lineage of being programmed with niches, chapels, or other sacred spaces.

iii

Kennecott Copper Mine, located in the southwest part of the Salt Lake Valley, is the largest open-pit copper mine in the world. In 1966, the mine was designated a National Historic Landmark under its original name, the Bingham Canyon Open Pit Copper Mine. It is currently owned by the multinational mining corporation Rio Tinto, which donated the copper for the exterior of the Saint Joseph the Worker day chapel.

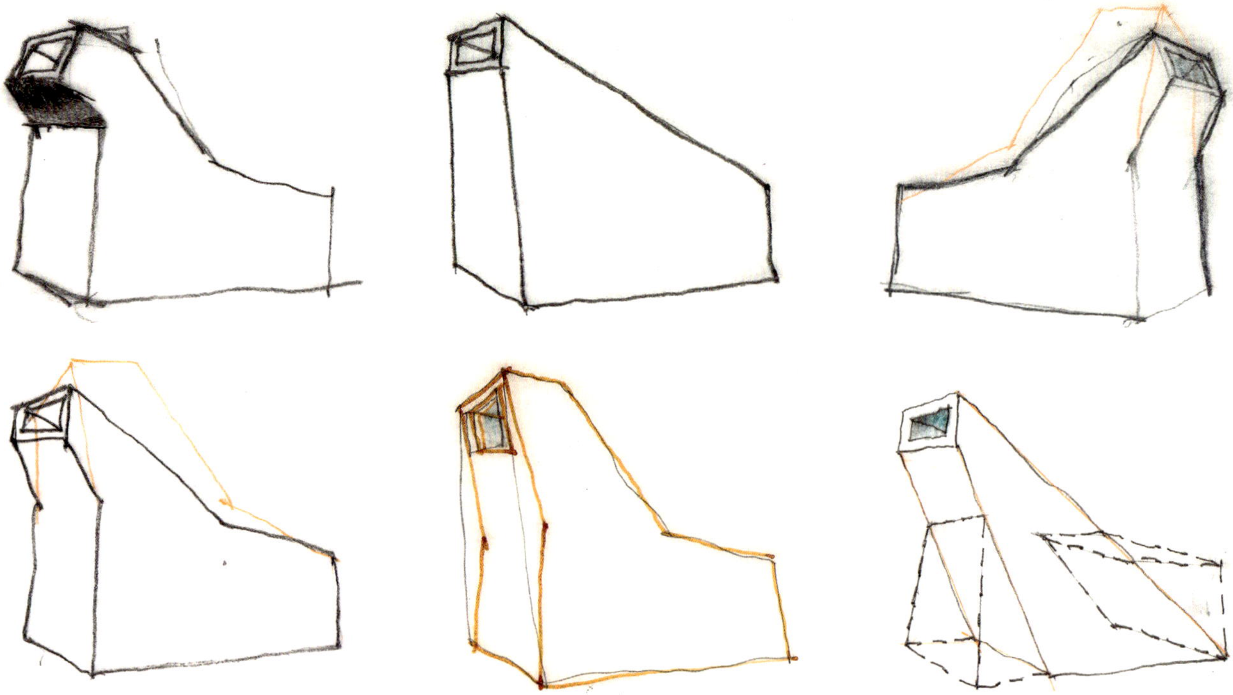

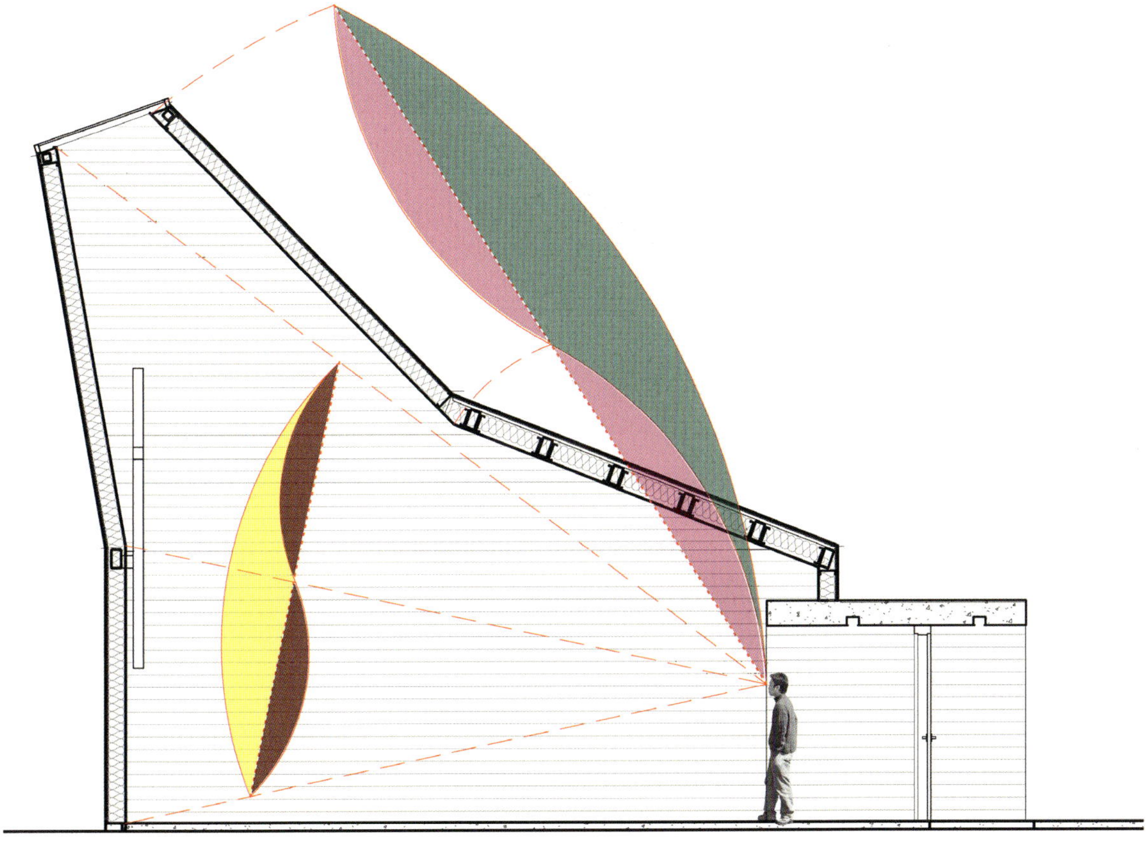

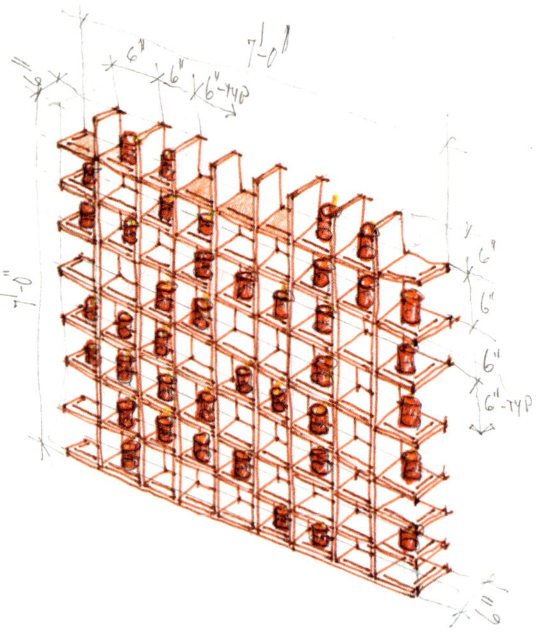
7'-0"
6"
6"
6"-TYP
7'-0"
6"
6"
6"
6"-TYP

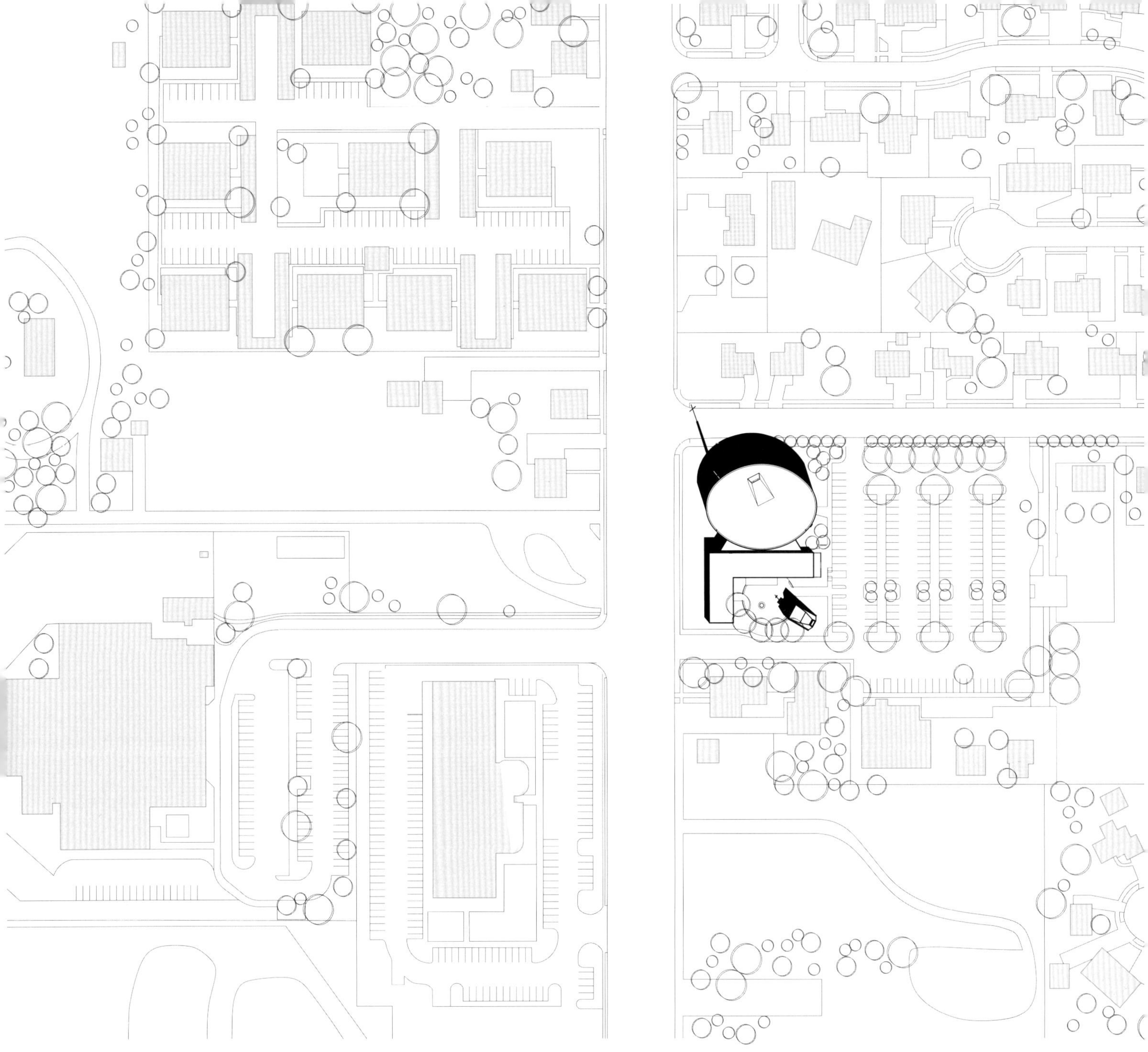

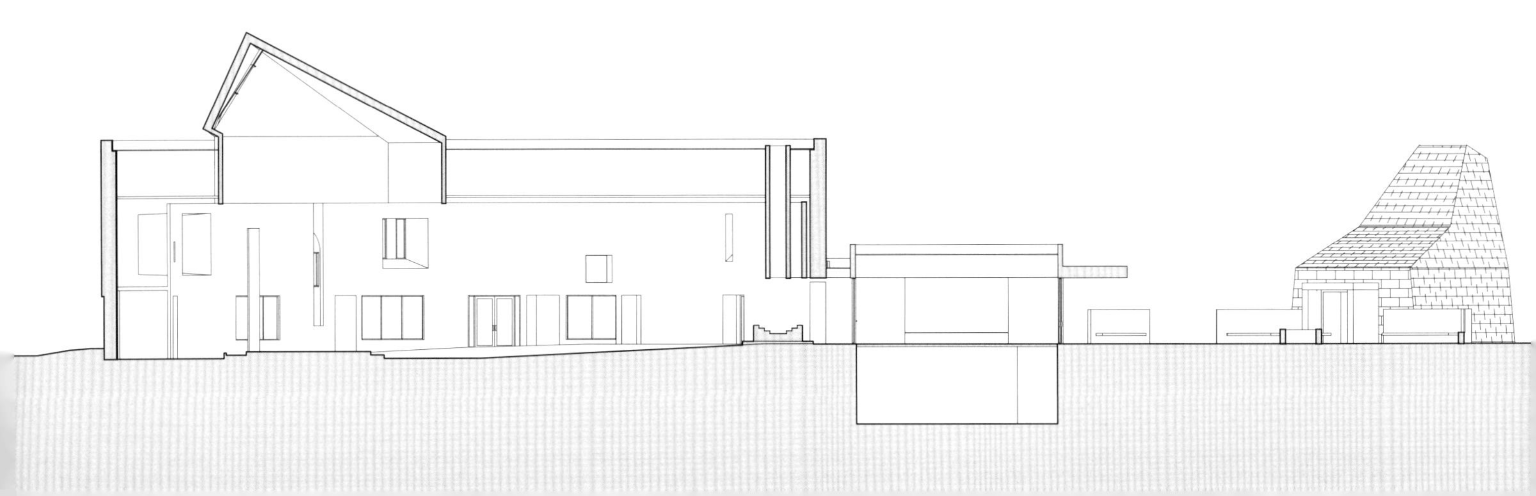

Main Level

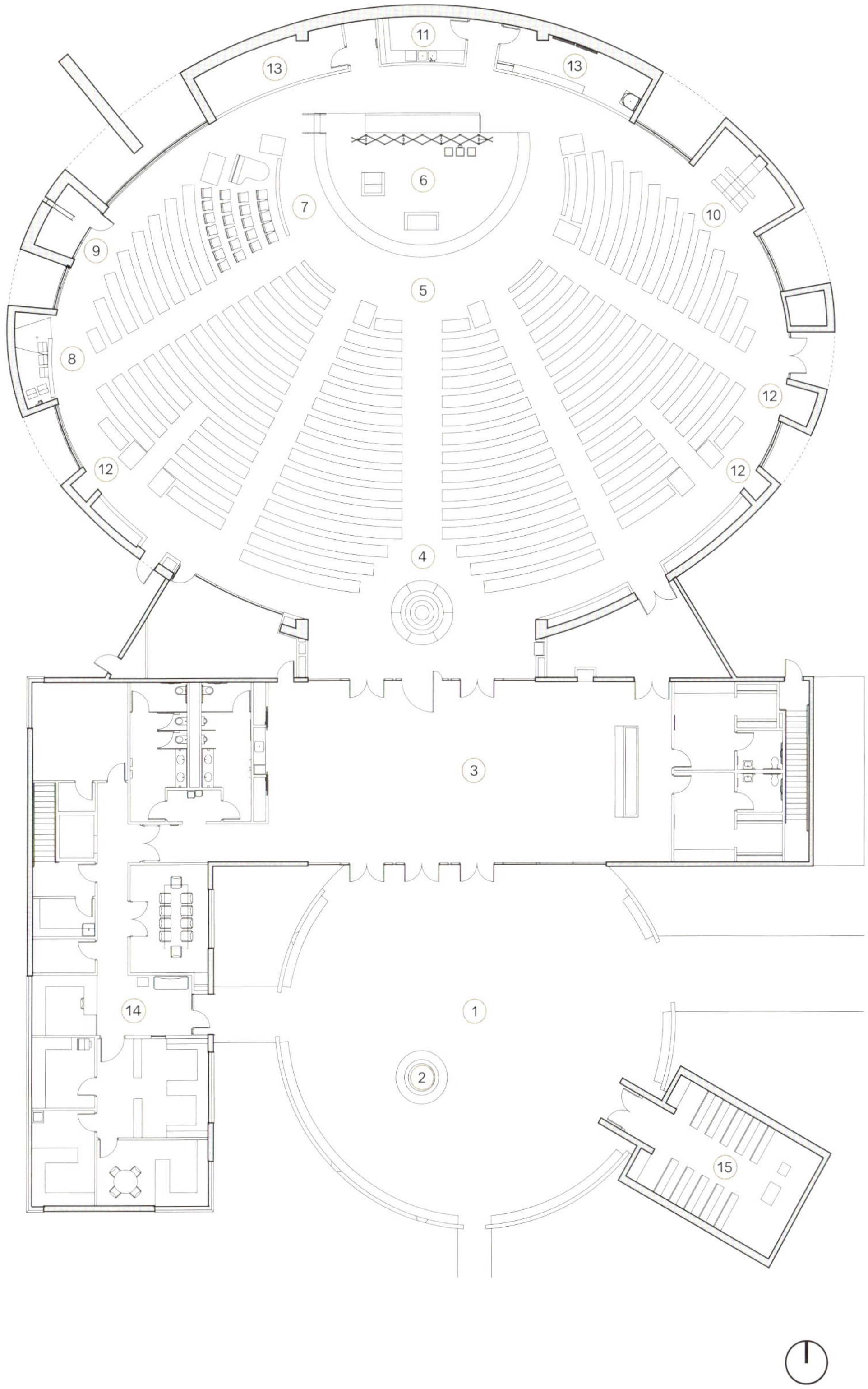

1 Courtyard
2 Water / Fire Feature
3 Gathering Space
4 Baptismal Font
5 Sanctuary
6 Altar
7 Choir
8 Prayer Niche
9 Chapel of Reconciliation
10 Chapel of the Blessed Sacrament
11 Sacristy
12 Niche
13 Storage
14 Clergy / Administration
15 Day Chapel

Image Captions

1 Construction image
2 Concept model
3 Massing studies; John Sparano
4 Design development sketches; John Sparano
5 Massing studies; John Sparano
6 Exterior from Redwood Road; © Jeremy Bittermann
7 Exterior facing south; © Jeremy Bittermann
8 Entrance to day chapel; © Jeremy Bittermann
Entrance into courtyard; © Jeremy Bittermann
Courtyard facing east; © Jeremy Bittermann
Exterior of day chapel; © Jeremy Bittermann
9 Day chapel massing studies; John Sparano
10 Day chapel entrance; © Jeremy Bittermann
11 Day chapel interior; © Jeremy Bittermann
12 Day chapel interior; © Jeremy Bittermann
Day chapel study model
Day chapel proportion study
13 Side chapel; © Jeremy Bittermann
14 Side chapel sketches; John Sparano
15 Main sanctuary sketches; John Sparano
16 Main sanctuary space; © Jeremy Bittermann
Stained-glass window studies
17 Stained-glass window from interior; © Scott Moses
18 Stained-glass windows; © Scott Moses
19 Concept sketch for candle niche; John Sparano
Prayer candle niche; © Jeremy Bittermann
20 Reconciliation screen (detail)
Reconciliation chapel
21 Exterior evening view; © Jeremy Bittermann
22 Site plan
Cross-section
23 Floor plan
Chipboard study model (detail)
Final model
Construction-in-progress; © Dana Sohm
24 Exterior (detail); © Scott Moses
25 Prayer candle chapel from sanctuary; © Jeremy Bittermann
View of main sanctuary from baptismal font; © Jeremy Bittermann
26 View of main sanctuary from altar; © Jeremy Bittermann

Completed 2010
Size 23,000 SF (2137m^2)
Location West Jordan, Utah

Owner/Client
Saint Joseph the Worker Parish (Father Patrick Carley, Pastor; Building Board, Ronald White, Chair)
Catholic Diocese of Salt Lake City

Team
John Sparano
Anne Mooney
Seth Striefel
Matthew Hintze
Soonju Kwon

Collaborators
McNeil Engineering (civil engineering)
Structural Design Studio (structural engineering)
Electrical Consulting Engineers (electrical engineering)
Colvin Engineering (mechanical engineering)
Spectrum Engineers (acoustical)
Landmark Design (landscape architects)

General Contractor
R&O Construction

Canyon House

Located in one of the seven canyons surrounding the Salt Lake Valley in Utah, this home offers a mountain refuge within easy reach of city life and amenities. To design an architecture for retreat requires a certain level of restraint, creating a simple structural form and leaving an open plan for flexible living. The design approach for this home celebrates the dynamic nature of domesticity with the idea that architecture can embody qualities of change and transformation over time.

The intertwined lines of an ancient Celtic symbol served as a guiding diagram for the design process.[i] This diagram can be interpreted as individual elements that, while interconnected, also exist independently and autonomously from one another. The house is grounded in an idea of domestic life as temporal, fleeting, and in continual flux. The resultant architecture creates a platform for experiences and connections to occur as lives are intertwined in space.

This design process led to the development of a topographic model. Its undulating forms with a superimposed system of thread floating above are disconnected from the landscape. Responding to the nature of domestic life, the architects created this web of interconnected elements as a superimposed field. This concept guided them to focus on ideas of change and the non-static possibilities of architecture, leading to an understanding of the home as a dynamic stage for living. Floor plans open to change and reconfiguration, along with a series of indoor-outdoor spaces connected to the natural context, were developed for the house.

This home captures expansive canyon views while offering a series of intimate gathering and entertainment spaces for the family. The interiors of the architecture are experienced through these framed views extending the space and providing a floor-to-ceiling canvas of visual art. The great room opens to unobstructed canyon views with a thirty-foot operable wall transforming the space into an outdoor room. Both the space and materiality of the house embody the theatrical. Domestic life, with changing roles and characters, plays out in areas evocative of a stage set, complete with curtain tracks inside and outside the glazed wall.

The architectural form is restrained, a simple abstract volume—nestled within its wooded site—clad in a shiny metal skin that, over time, takes on a mottled surface, eventually settling into a thick rusted skin of red-brown. The transformation of this Corten skin marks time just as the home's inhabitants expand, contract, age, and experience change.[ii] The home was designed for aging in place and offers long-term flexibility, including a lower-floor multiuse space for guests, caregivers, a home office, playroom, or art studio.

As we lament the loss of craft traditions in our culture, this project celebrates making, visible in the skilled application of interlocking shingles forming the building wrapper. For weeks on-site, during heat, rain, sleet, and snow, a dedicated metalworker practiced his trade as he expertly joined and applied the folded shiny cladding. Its coppery color eventually tuned itself to match the leaves of the surrounding scrub oak trees each fall. This Corten steel cladding is combined with a board-formed wood-textured concrete and glass for a contextual and low-maintenance material palette.

The design required minimum excavation of the site and allowed for the retention of much of the native oak. The house earned the first LEED Silver home certification in the state.[iii] Its small footprint, heated floors, rainwater catchment, super-insulated walls, and drought-tolerant and native vegetation minimize the home's environmental impact. The residents are beekeepers and organic gardeners, and gather their firewood from the site, further linking the home's inhabitants to their canyon location. Daylight streams into all rooms through expansive glazing and solar tube skylights. Warmth is provided through an energy-efficient in-floor radiant heating system.

i

The triskelion is an ancient symbol consisting of three interlocking spirals emanating from a single point. Although this motif appears in many cultures, it is most closely associated with Celtic and Gaelic traditions. The symbol is carved into the entrance of Newgrange in County Meath, Ireland, and a version of it, composed of three legs, is found in Greek and Italian cultural artifacts and appears on the flag of Sicily.

ii

Corten is a steel alloy material that forms a stable rusted surface after exposure to the elements. It was developed to eliminate the need for finishes with its protective layer of rust, which continuously regenerates.

iii

LEED (Leadership in Energy and Environmental Design) for homes is a rating system for the design and construction of high-performance buildings. It is a certification process from the United States Green Building Council with points for incorporating principles of sustainable design and energy and resource efficiency, and for enhancing the quality of indoor environments.

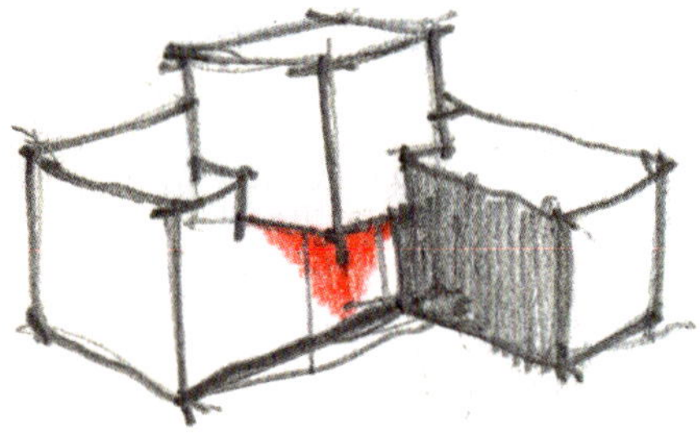

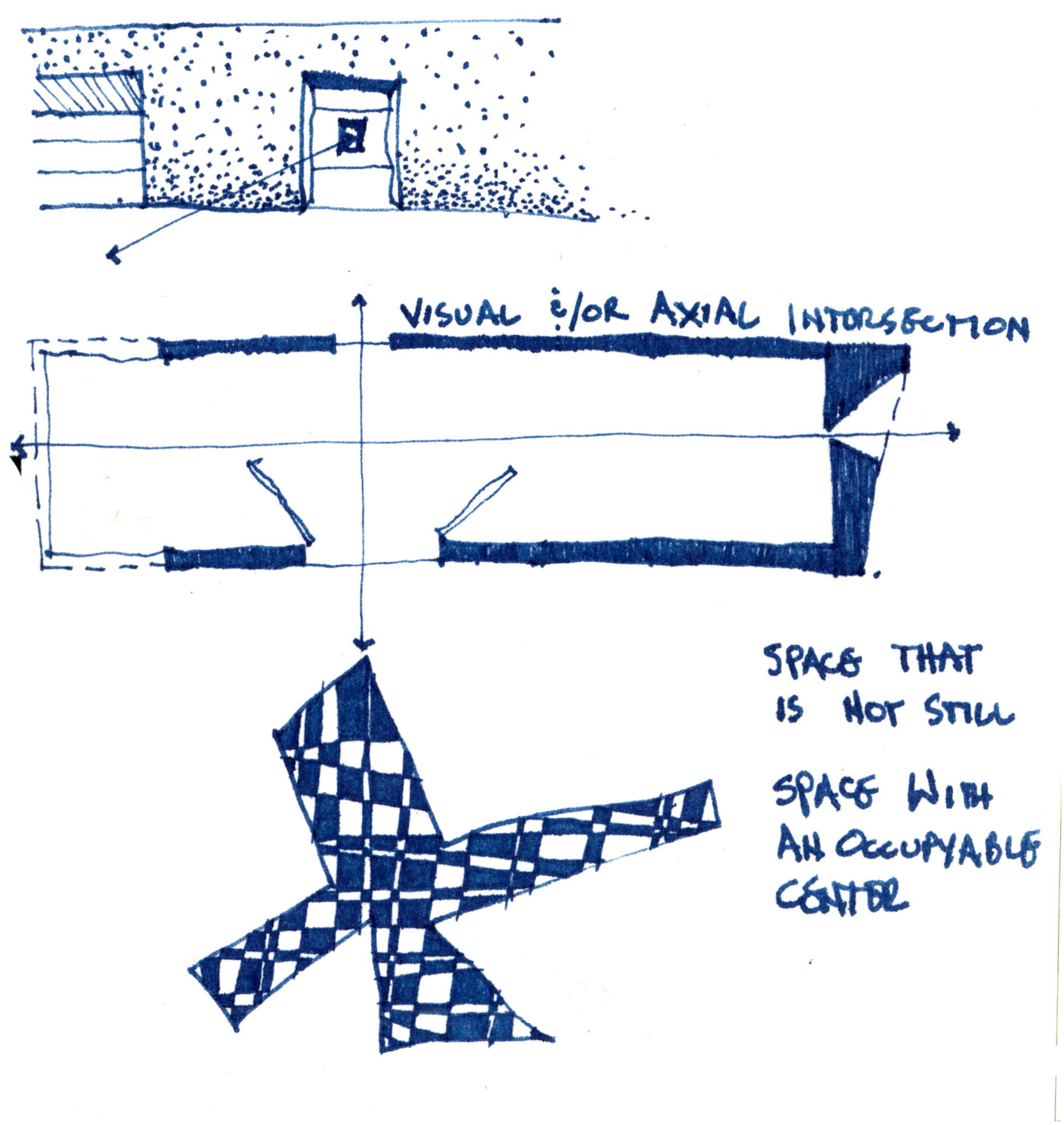
VISUAL &/OR AXIAL INTERSECTION
SPACE THAT IS NOT STILL
SPACE WITH AN OCCUPYABLE CENTER

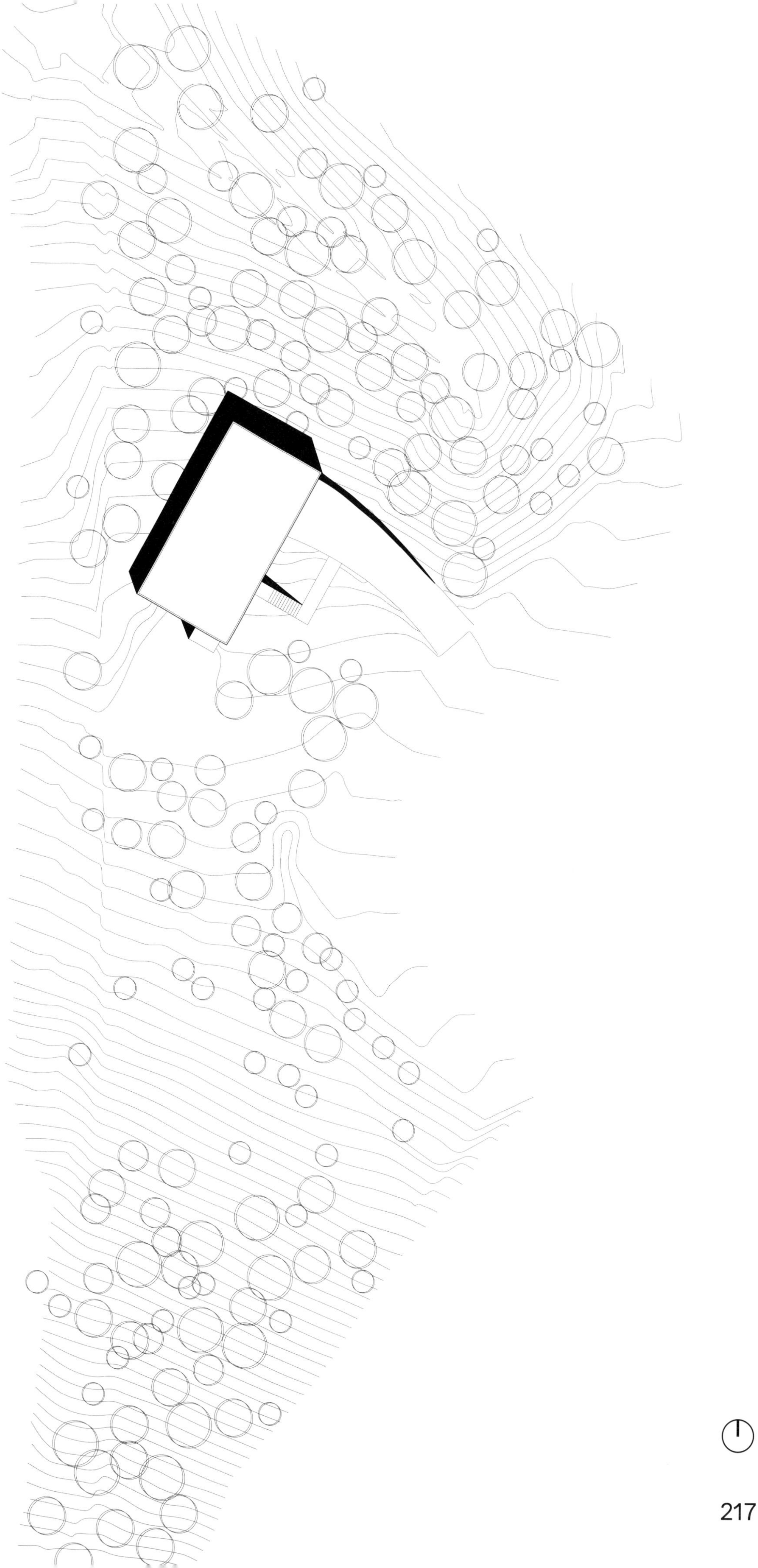

Image Captions		
	1	Exterior
	2	Concept sketches; John Sparano
	3	Concept sketches; John Sparano
	4	Massing study sketches; John Sparano
	5	Exterior view
	6	Great room with open window; © Denis Mecham
	7	Exterior view
	8	Porch and stair Exterior stair (detail)
	9	North facade
	10	East facade (detail) Exterior stair (detail)
	11	Fireplace and wood storage; © Dustin Aksland Final model
	12	Winter view of exterior; © Bryan Allen
	13	Corten cladding (detail)
	14	Site plan
	15	Exterior night view; © Bryan Allen

Completed	2009
Size	2,500 SF (232 m²)
Location	Emigration Canyon, Utah
Team	John Sparano Anne Mooney Seth Striefel
Collaborators	Dunn Engineers (structural engineering) McNeil Engineering (civil engineering)
General Contractor	Benchmark

Kimball Art Center

Sparano + Mooney Architecture designed the Kimball Art Center as part of an international invited competition to reimagine this museum and event and art education center located in the heart of Park City, Utah. The design, inspired by aspen trees growing in the surrounding mountain range, reflects the organization's mission to serve as the center of a thriving, connected creative community.[i] The design concepts, rooted in the center's past, were intended to provide future generations with a heightened awareness of sustainable design, energy production and consumption, and environmental conditions unique to the Mountain West, including the problem of beetle kill deforestation.[ii]

The design process involved two complementary investigations: the first involved an exploration of the center's culture, mission, and programs, and a site analysis of its prominent corner location in the heart of Park City. This research provided the basis of the conceptual framework for the project and led to the *parti* diagram inspired by the aspen tree. The networked roots of the aspen trees serve conceptually as a thriving underground metaphor for an architectural foundation from which programmed spaces emerge. Surrounding these program activities is the building's tree canopy: an etched, triple-glazed photovoltaic screen forming a dynamic circulation space filled with filtered daylight and generating energy for the center.

The second focus of the design investigation led to the development of a unified relationship among the architecture, exhibition and education spaces, and the visitor experience. This connection was achieved by creating an intuitive circulation system woven through the building, punctuated by a series of dynamic experiences unfolding along its path. The process of crafting memories for visitors as they move from space to space and floor to floor, actively engaging with the architecture, brings a fresh perspective to the creation and display of artwork, and to experiencing the unique mountain setting.

The center's aspen-etched screen building wrapper embodies the qualities of transformation through its ability to change from day to night. Looking through the screen offers dynamic views of the mountains and activity on the street. The idealized Western vernacular log architecture is also present in the project within its central volume, evocative of a cabin surrounded by aspen woods. Public spaces are animated with textural walls graphically depicting the image of trees damaged by bark beetles and salvaged from Utah's Wasatch mountain range.

The design creates a highly flexible creative hub able to meet the needs of a diverse constituency within its thirty-five-thousand square feet. The building serves as a cultural center, a community center, an educational facility, an exhibition space, an event space and world stage, a workplace, and a memorable place to visit during the annual Sundance Film Festival.[iii] The architecture offers a balance of these diverse program zones while providing a dialogue between spaces through layering and the sensitive manipulation of materials and light. The lower level contains vibrant education and support spaces, including community art studios. The main floor operates as a civic plaza welcoming the public into the center and its café, retail, and commercial spaces, with all elements easily accessible and visible from the street.

The floor plan is organized with a perimeter circulation system, moving visitors from floor to floor while providing glimpses into creative studios and galleries, and out to the city, mountains, and sky. The exhibition spaces are flexible enough for events, large or small, including lectures, film screenings, receptions, or dinners. Access, acoustics, and lighting are controlled in zones, allowing up to four events to be held simultaneously. There are two rooftop classroom, exhibition, and event zones served by restroom and catering facilities. The art center spaces are easily transformed into world-class galleries and event venues, but also operate as one-of-a-kind environments for visitors to experience in Park City.

i

Utah is home to Pando, a massive colony of the quaking aspen tree, consisting of 47,000 genetically identical trees connected by a single root system. This colony is one of the largest living organisms on the planet and was studied for its interconnected structure and ability to share resources within its vast network.

ii

The bark beetle has thrived in western states after decades of drought and warming temperatures made conifer forests in North America more susceptible to infestation. Since 1990, the US Forest Service's Rocky Mountain Research Station has documented millions of trees killed annually by the bark beetle.

iii

Sundance Film Festival is the largest independent film festival in the United States. This annual event brings over 100,000 visitors to Utah to celebrate independent filmmakers and diverse expressions of film.

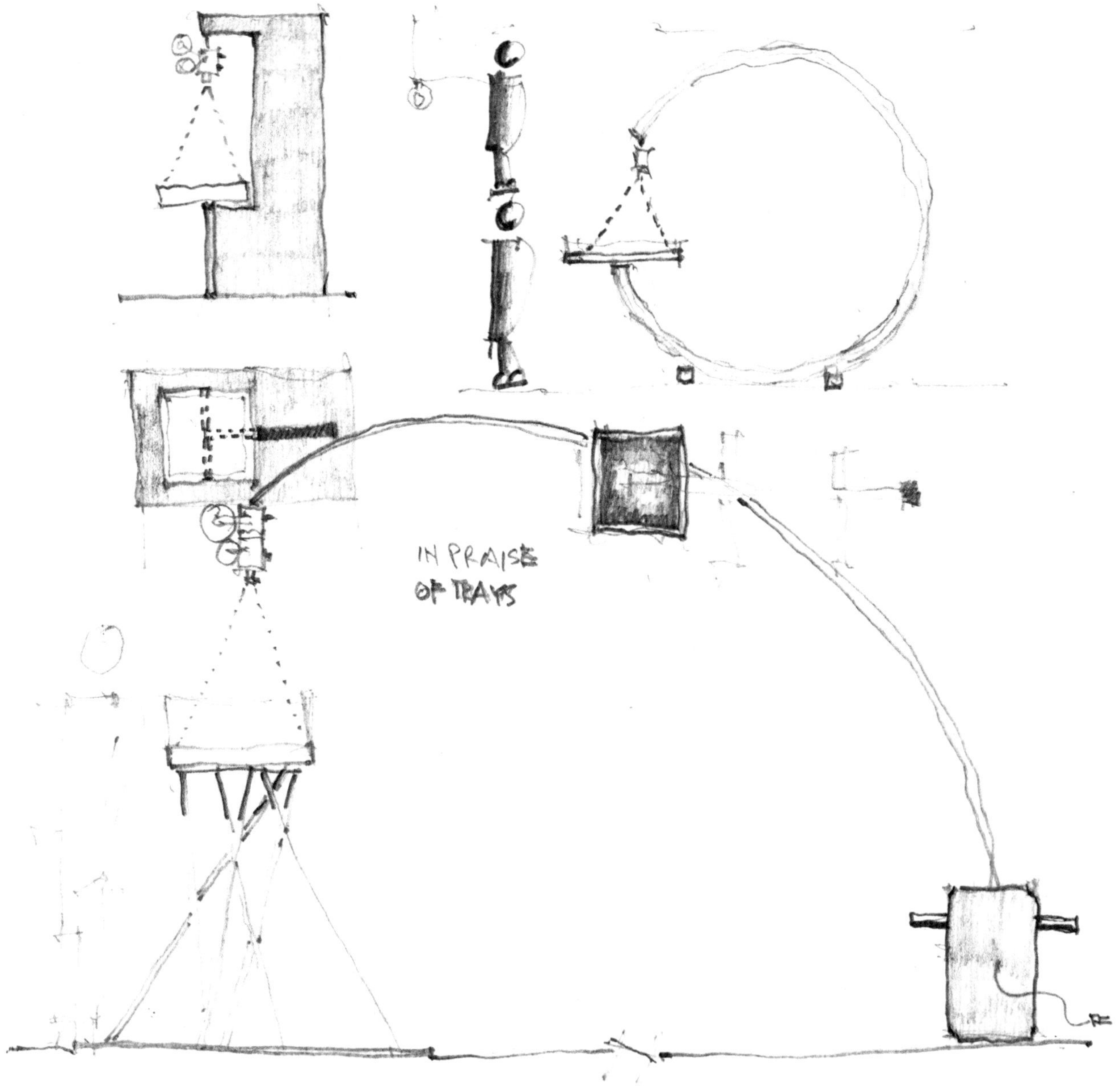
IN PRAISE
OF TRAYS

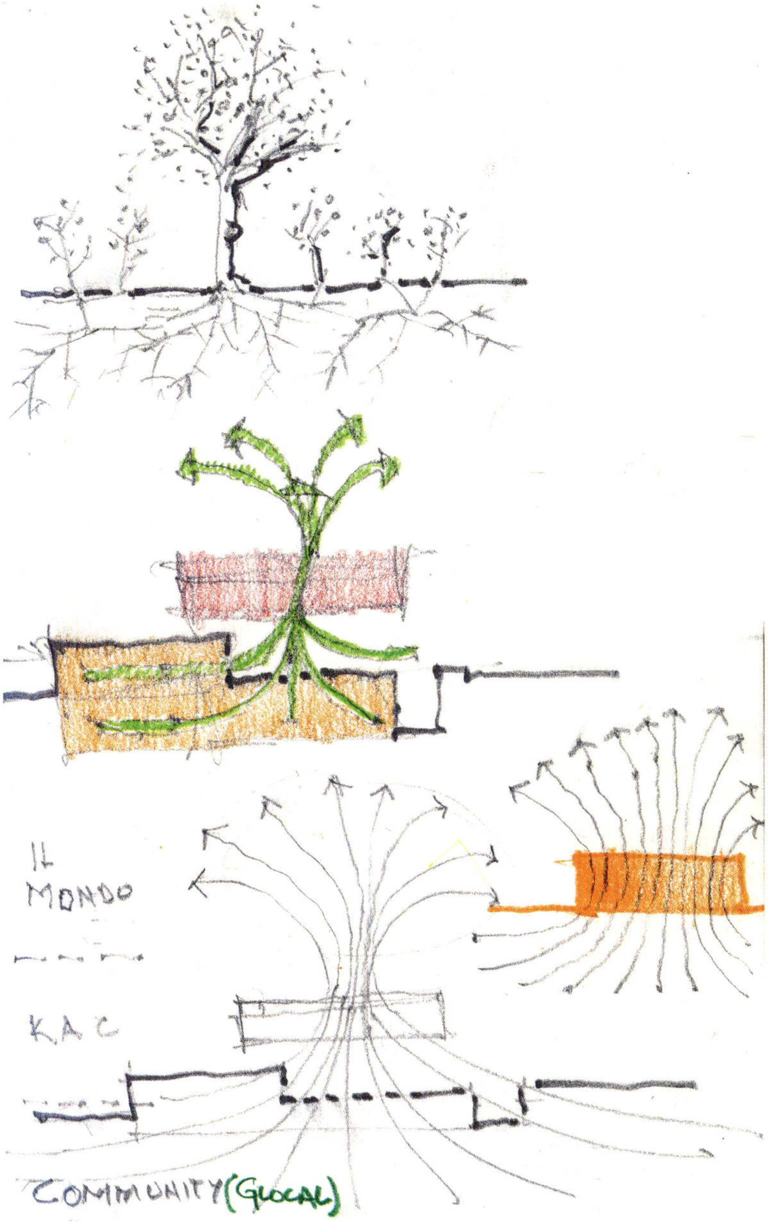
IL
MONDO
K.A.C
COMMUNITY(GLOCAL)

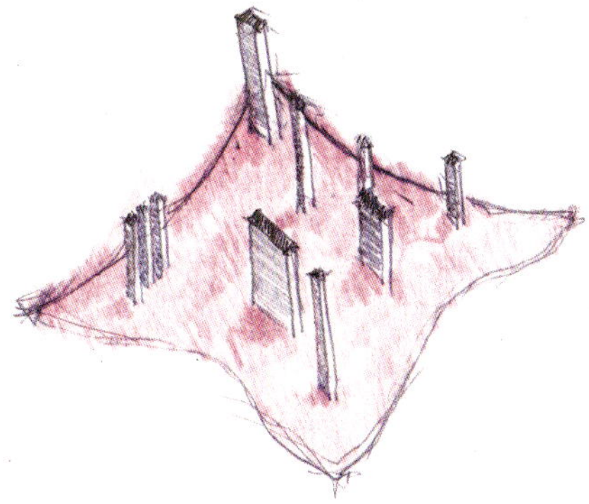

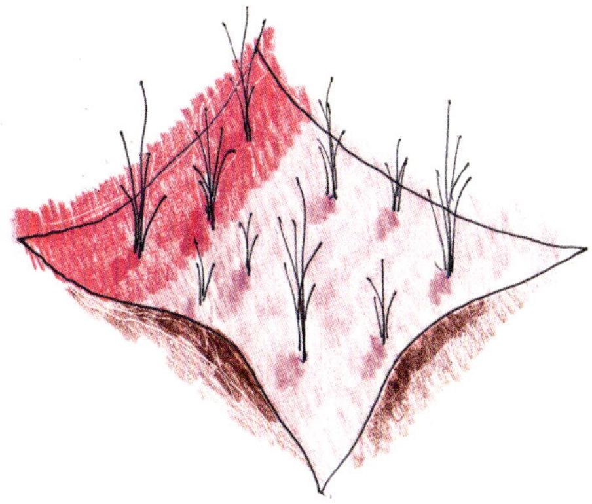

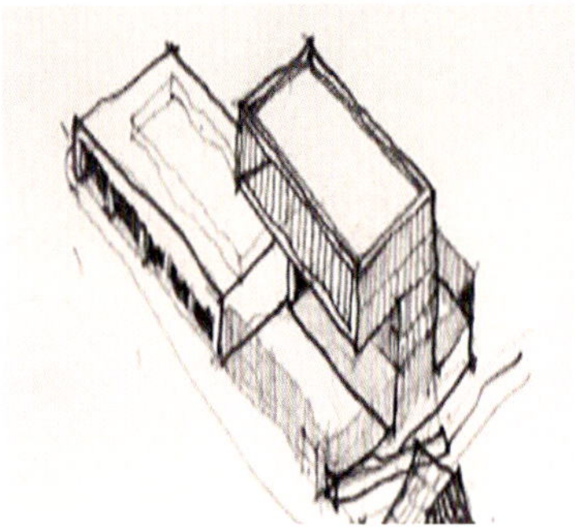

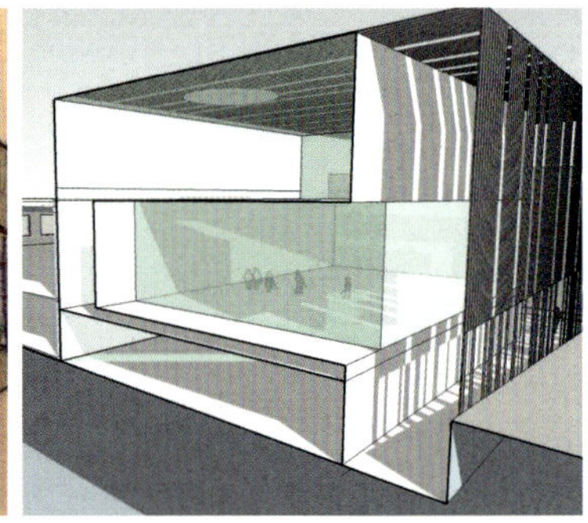
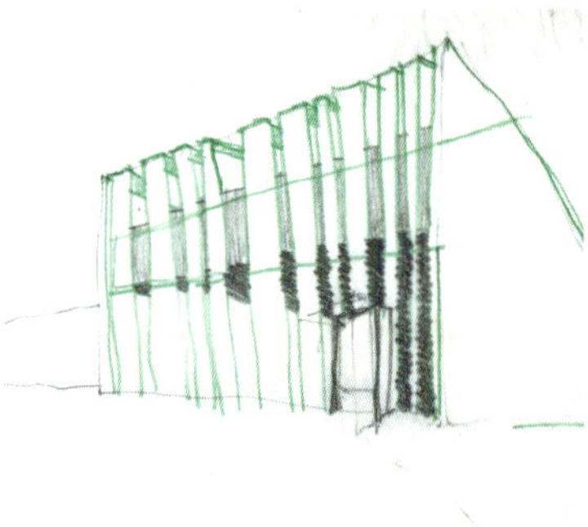

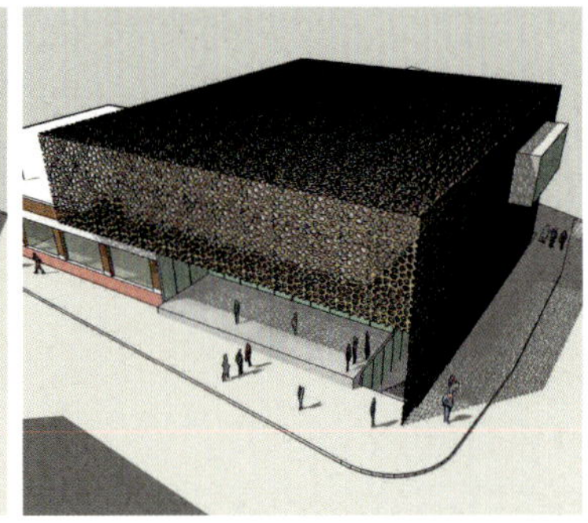
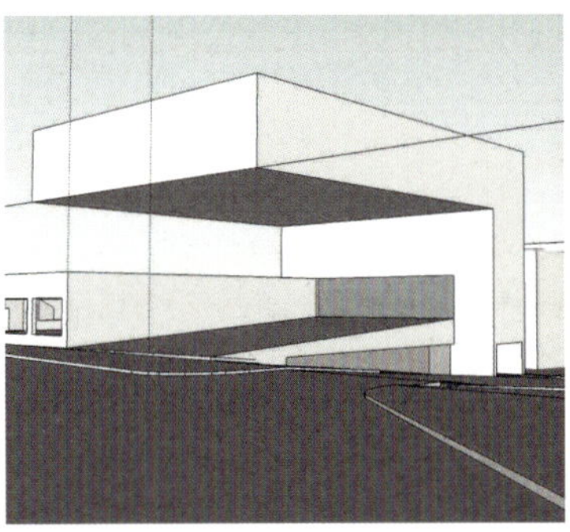

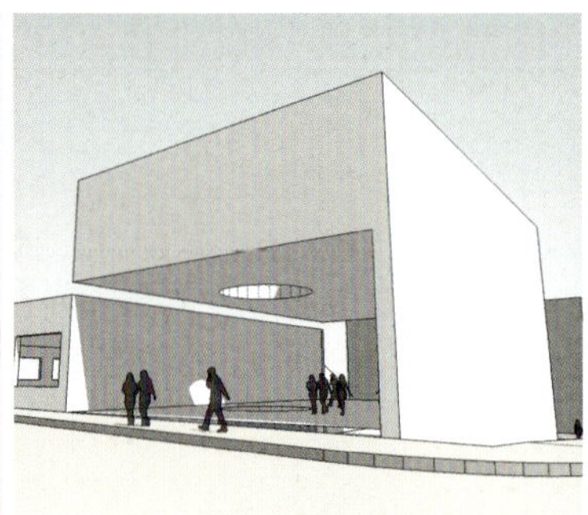
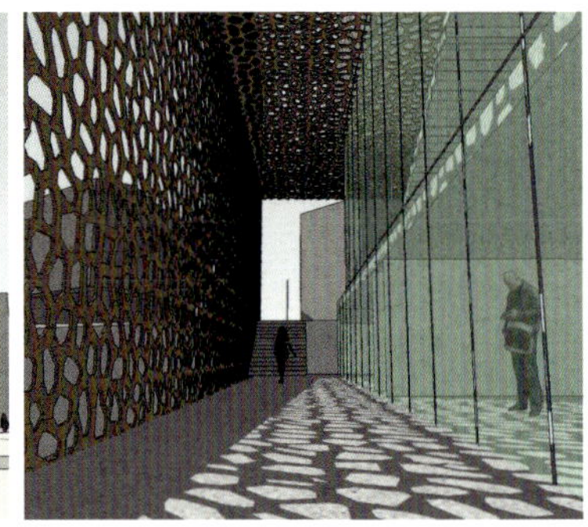

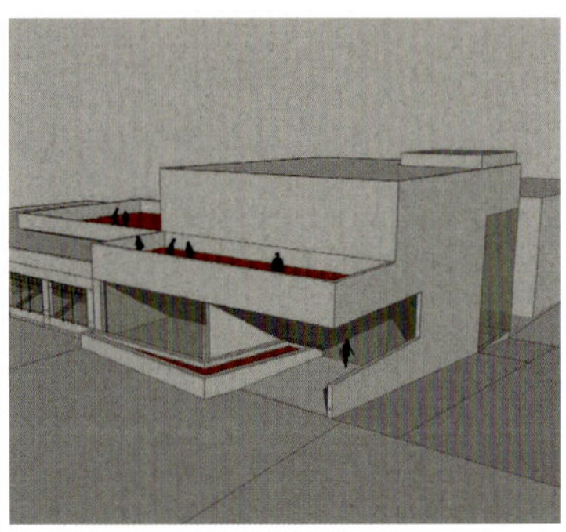
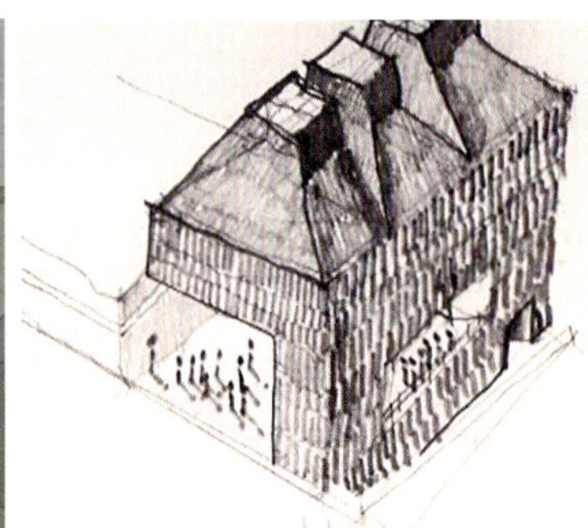
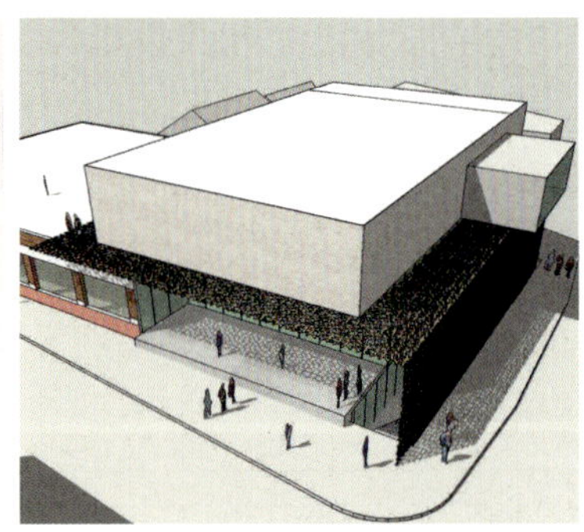

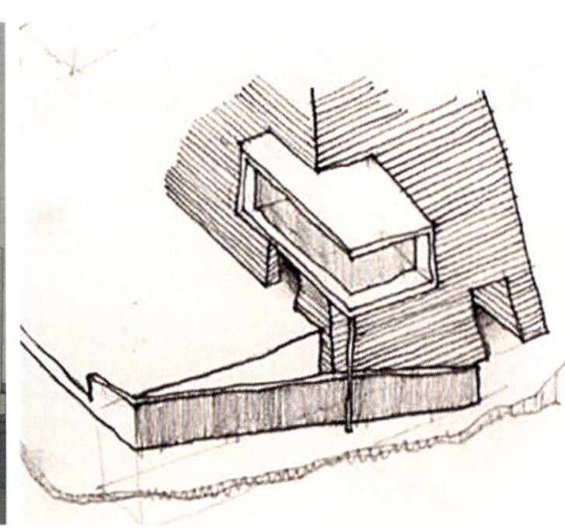

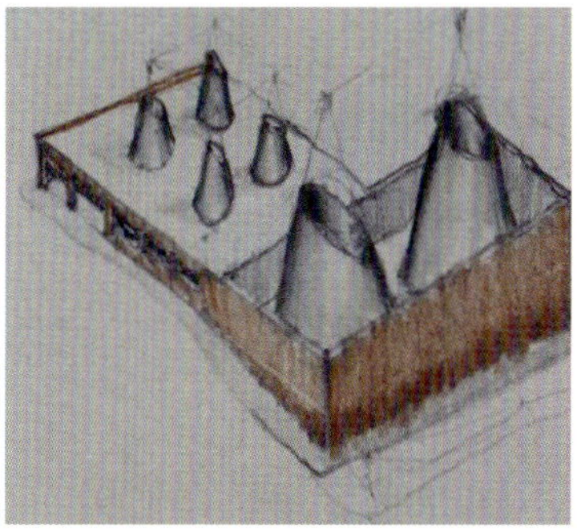
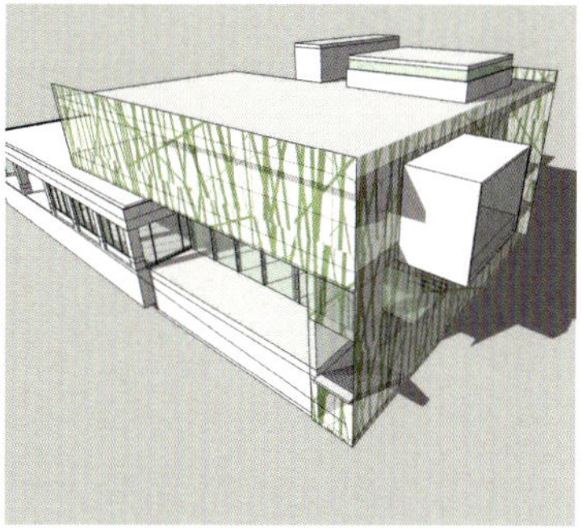

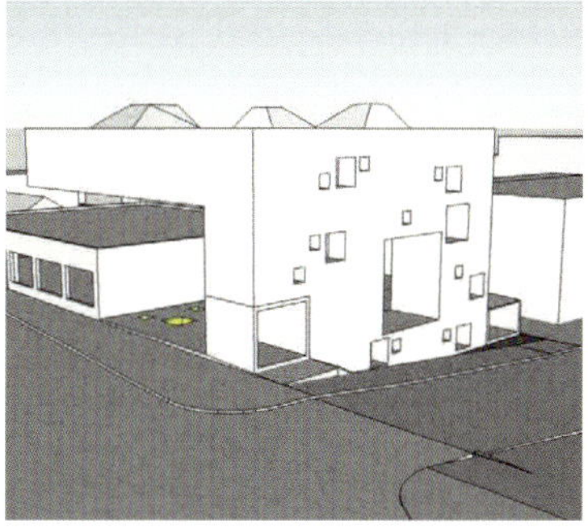

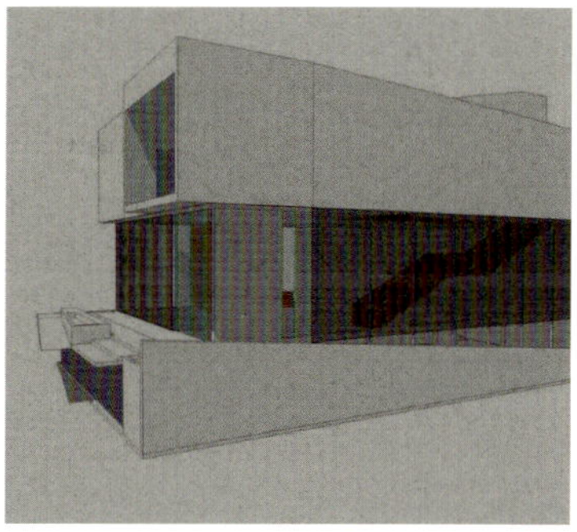

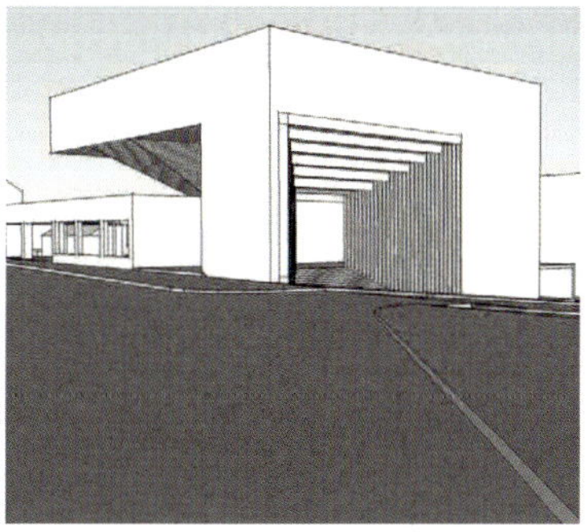

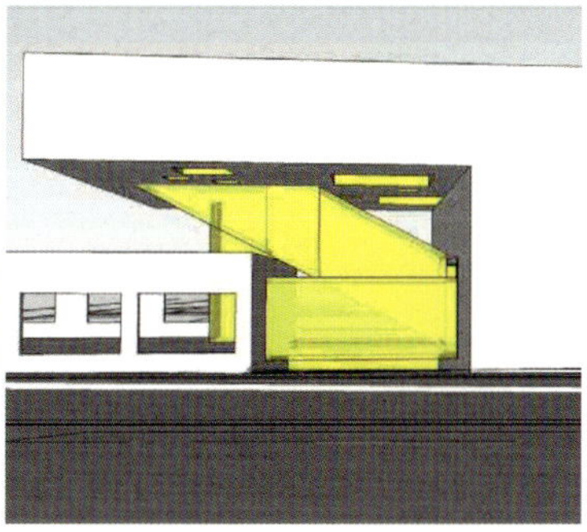

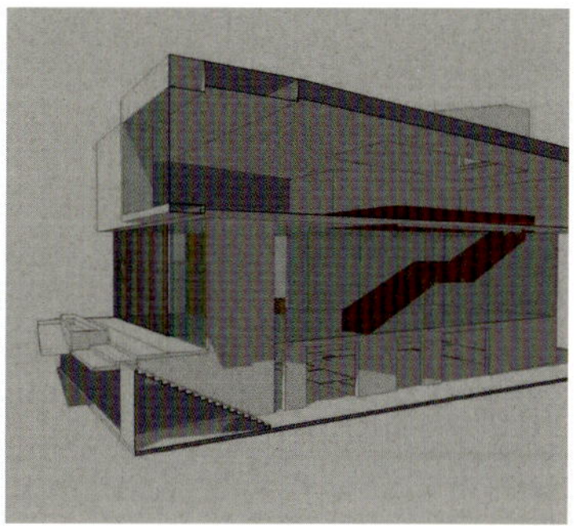

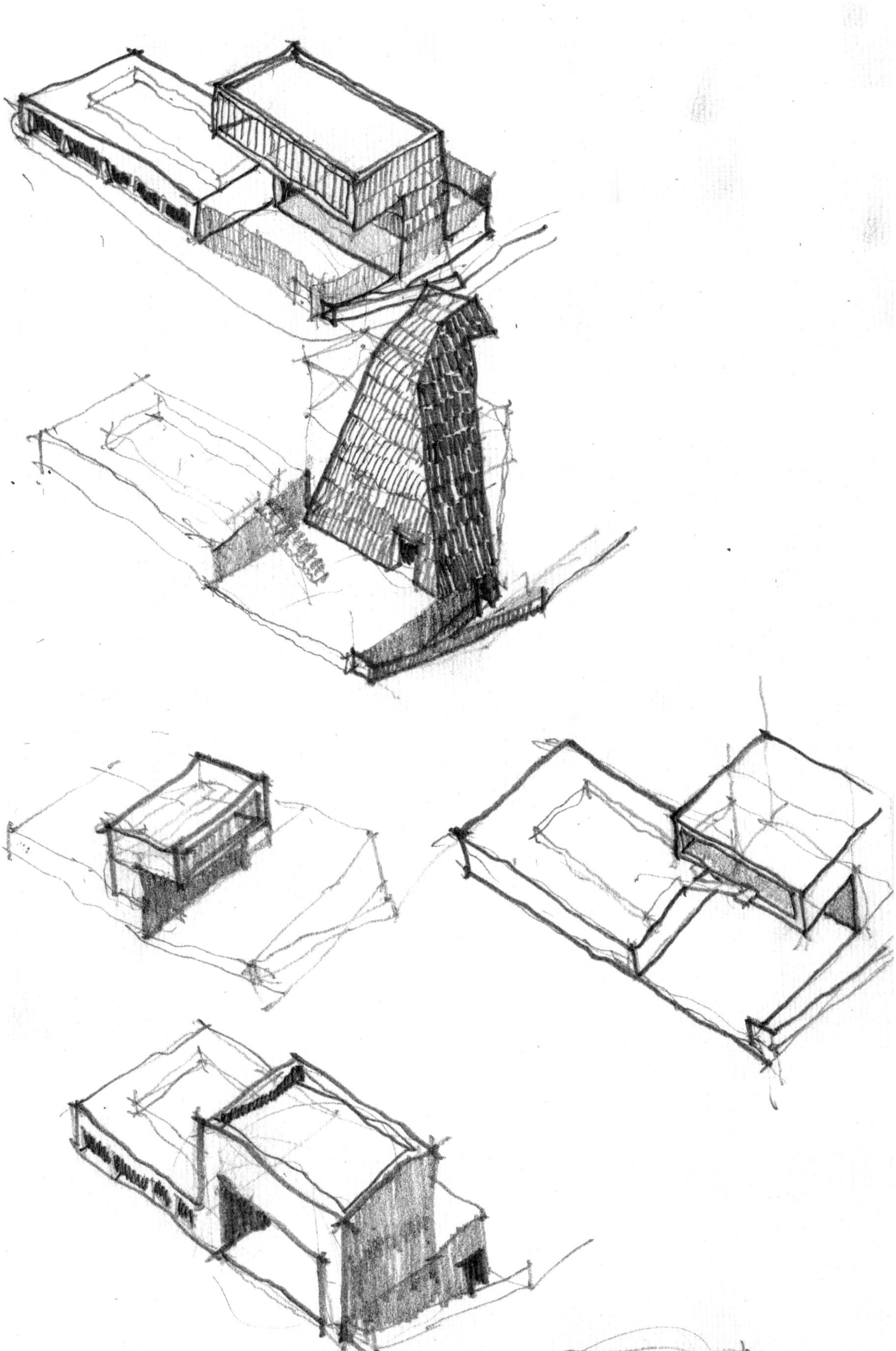

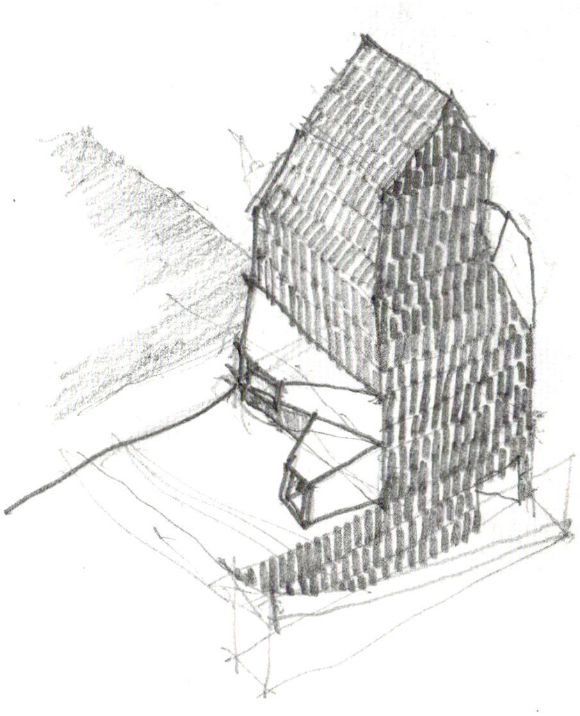

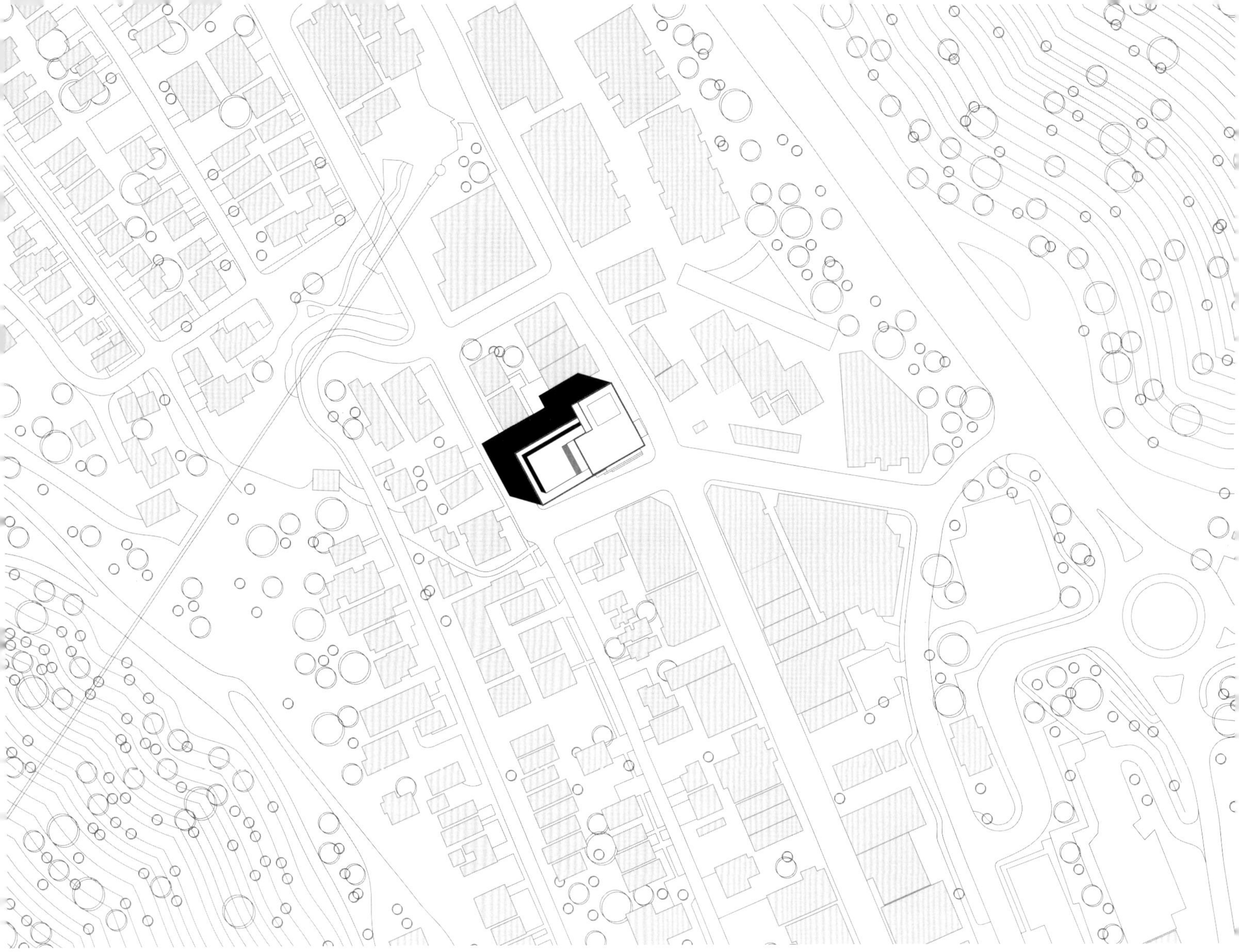

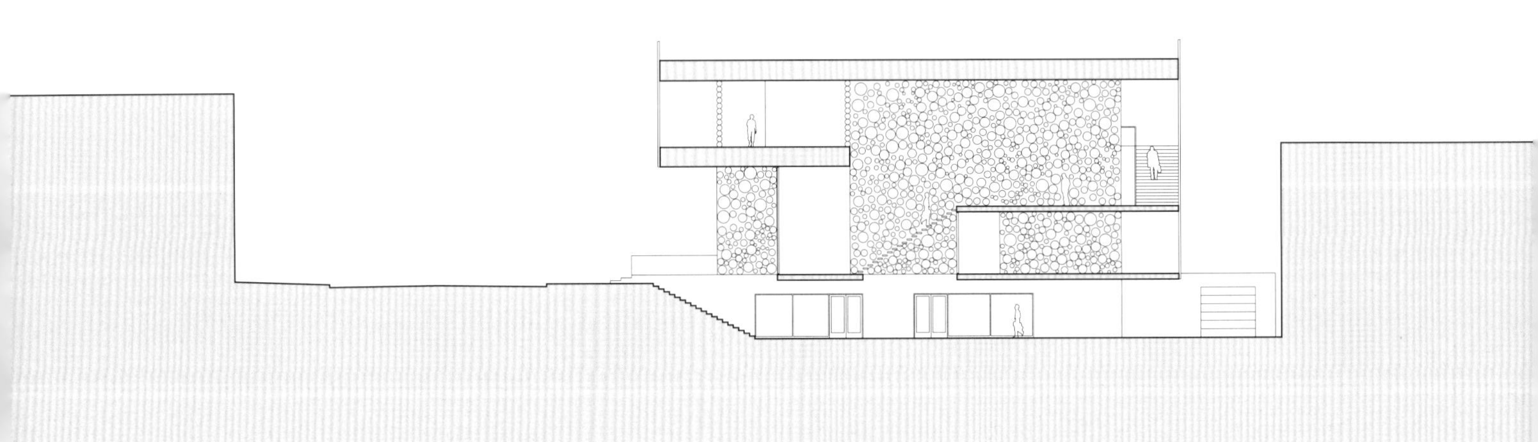

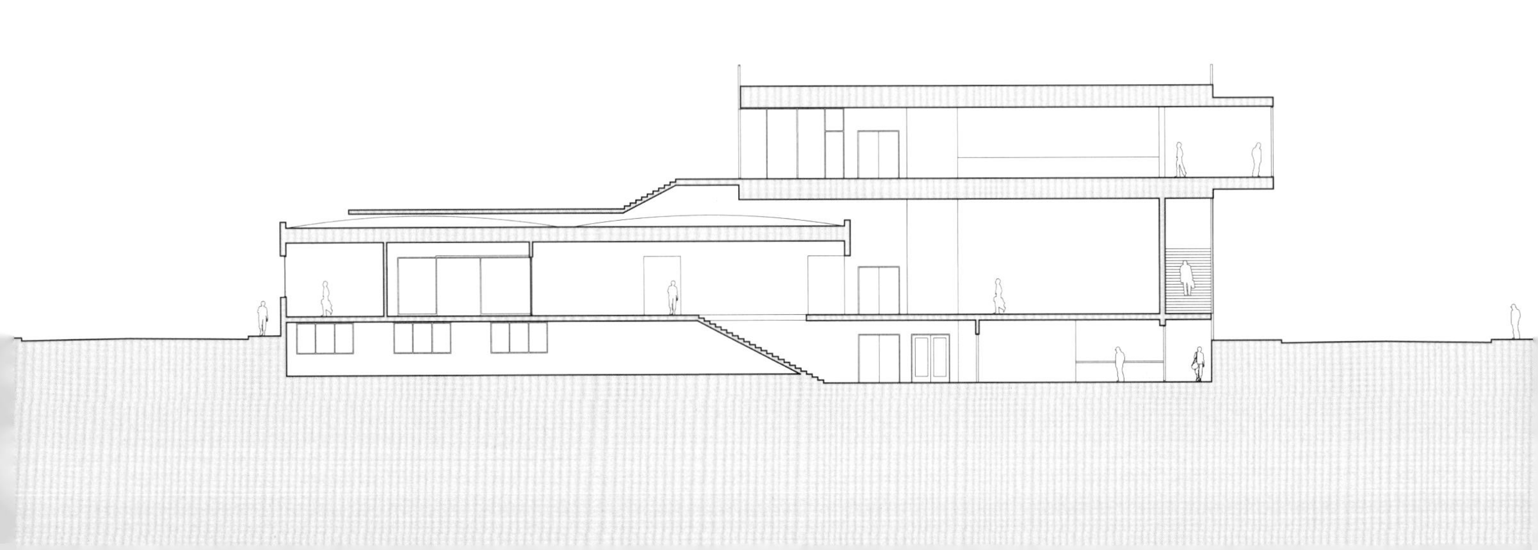

Upper Level

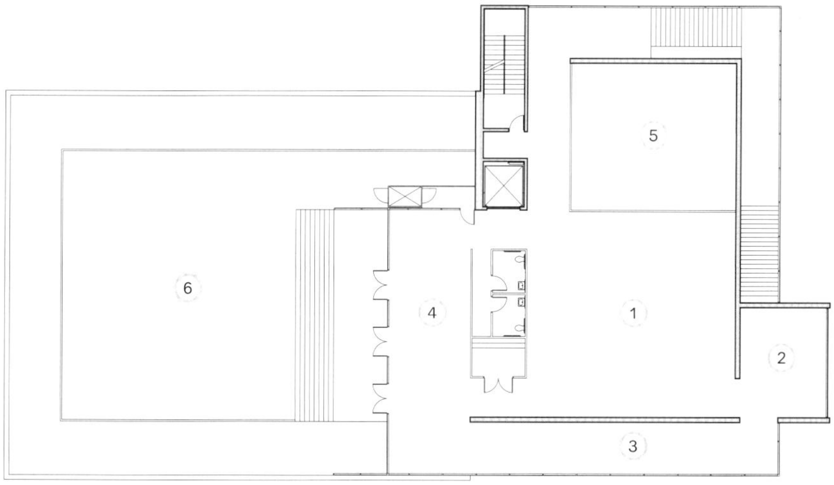

1 Main Gallery / Event Space
2 Classroom / Screening Room
3 Linear Gallery
4 Gallery
5 Open to Below
6 Rooftop Deck

Street Level

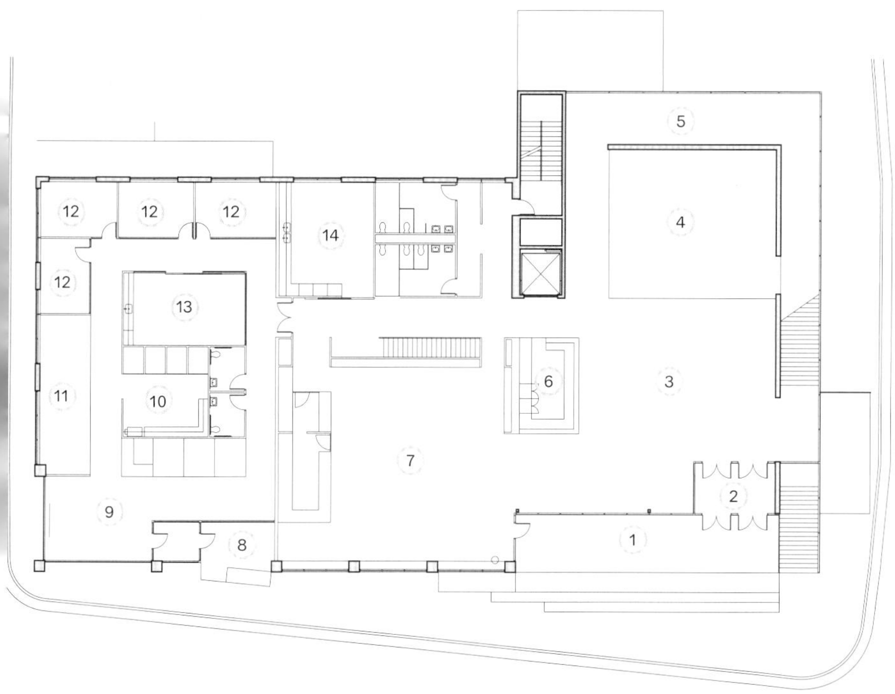

1 Entry Plaza
2 Main Entry
3 Lobby / Event Space
4 Gallery Event Space (Open to Above)
5 Linear Gallery
6 Reception
7 Café / Event Space / Music Venue
8 Admin Entry
9 Admin Reception
10 Printing Room
11 Open Work Area
12 Office
13 Conference Room
14 Catering Kitchen

Lower Level

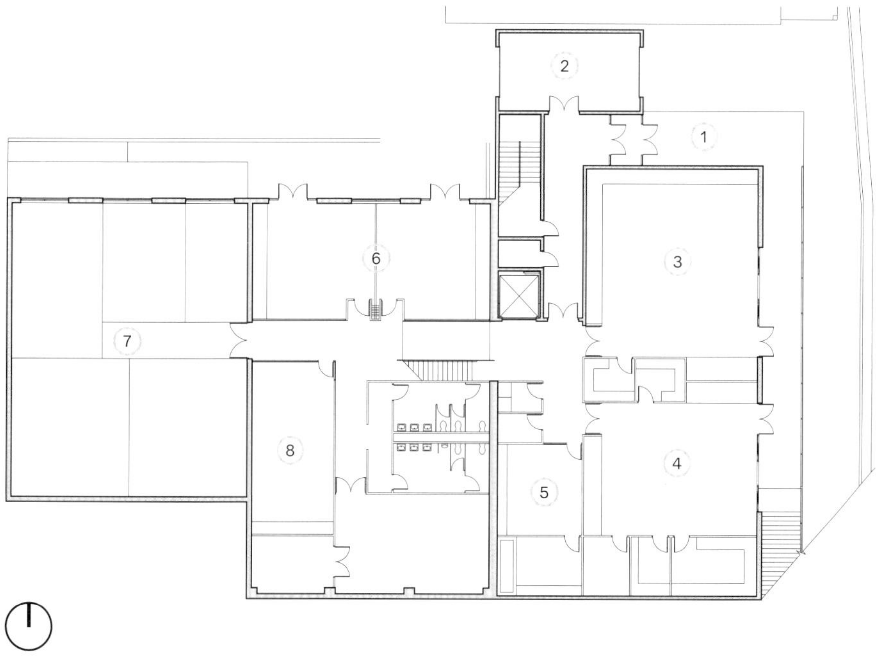

1 Education / Studio Entry
2 Shipping and Receiving
3 Welding / Smithing / Glass Studio
4 Ceramic Studio
5 Photo Lab
6 Adult and Youth Studios
7 Workshop Storage
8 Digital Studio

Image Captions

1 Stairway rendering
2 Concept sketches; John Sparano
3 Concept sketches; John Sparano
Heuristic device
4 Massing studies
5 Massing studies
6 Design process materials
7 Exterior rendering, night view
8 Exterior rendering, day view
9 Massing study sketches; John Sparano
10 Upper gallery view
Massing study sketch; John Sparano
Street view of studio space
11 Site plan
Cross-section
Longitudinal section
12 Upper-level floor plan
Street-level floor plan
Lower-level floor plan
13 View of roof deck
14 Lobby right rendering

Completed	2011
Size	35,000 SF (3252 m^2)
Location	Park City, Utah
Team	John Sparano Anne Mooney Seth Striefel Matthew Hintze Marco Colaiacomo Ludwing Juraez Jorge Beltran
Collaborators	Plastik Banana / Brad Brinton Design Workshop (model)

Wabi-Sabi

Wabi-sabi,[i] an ancient tenet of Japanese aesthetic culture, is a philosophy that embraces the imperfect, the incomplete, and the transient. *Wabi-sabi* espouses simplicity and honesty in expression and the beauty of things as they weather and age. In exploring the mountain setting for this home, the architects were moved by the way light changes dramatically over time, illuminating the undulating grooves in the bark of the surrounding oak and stone shards on the site. The design process for the Wabi-Sabi house began to coalesce around ideas of texture, light, materials, and expressive joinery and connections.

The architecture is expressed as two volumes floating above the landscape, grounded in the earth as they are joined together forming the entrance. The north volume is oriented along an east-west axis and contains the private functions of the residence with quiet mountain views to the north. The southwest volume contains the public spaces with dramatic views to the city below. Rather than cutting deeply into the site, the architects opted to float the house above the land. The site anchors and connects eighteen- and twenty-four-foot cantilevers hovering over the earth, minimally disturbing the native landscape.

Located directly adjacent to a nature preserve, the site was planned to maintain animal game paths and hiking and mountain-biking trails. The home celebrates its uniquely elevated canyon location, offering direct access to nature. It is oriented to capture dramatic city views from the great room and frame a secluded mountain overlook from the primary suite. Steeply sloped terrain spectacularly frames nighttime valley views of the twinkling city lights below. The architecture is an expression of both static and dynamic elements on the site and references the relationship of the mountain to its seasonally changing landscape and wildlife habitat.

Once inside, visitors move down a set of stairs to the great room, which opens to unobstructed canyon views. Along the way, slatted screened walls offer fragmented views of the site and surroundings. Skylights light the path running the full length of the volume, illuminating a textural art wall. Materials reflecting the site express constructed connections and detailing. The porous wood entry screen provides glimpses into the home and back out to the landscape. This fragmented surface folds into solid wood cladding. Its textural rain screen changes slowly over time, weathering first into a brighter, warm russet, then settling into a silvery gray. The approach to materials extends to the selection of interior elements, fixtures, and accessories, each emphasizing joinery and craft.

The home offers the family a dramatic experience of the four seasons, with its outdoor spaces intimately connected to key interiors. These indoor/outdoor relationships are created through large openings onto exterior concrete plinths in alignment with the site's topography. The interior great room fireplace is mirrored on axis by an outdoor fireplace, both creating space for family and friends to gather. A vegetated roof planted with local grasses also serves to embed the home sensitively within its context.

i
Description of *wabi-sabi* is from *In Praise of Shadows* by Jun'ichiro Tanizaki (Vintage Classics: England, 2001).

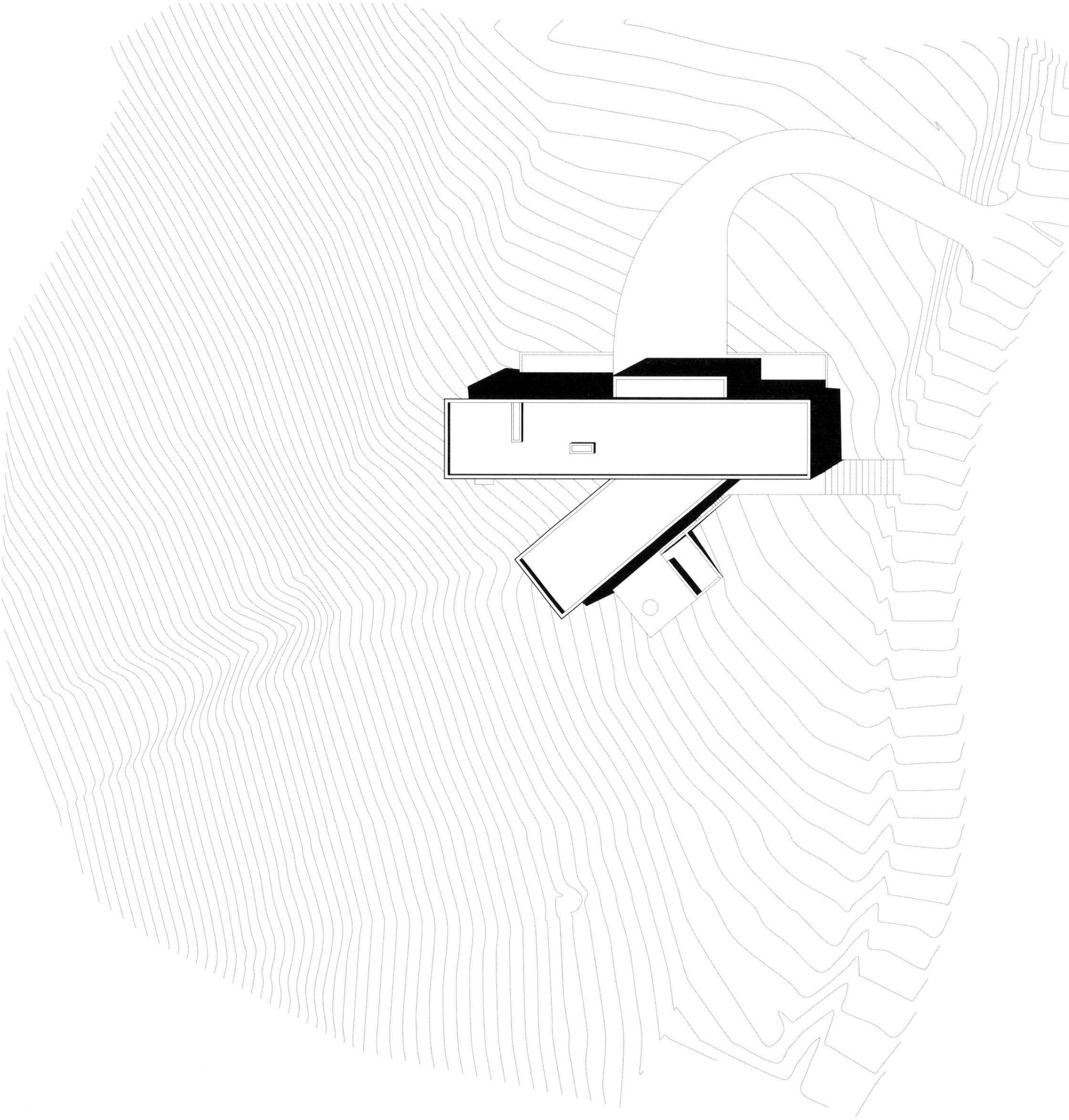

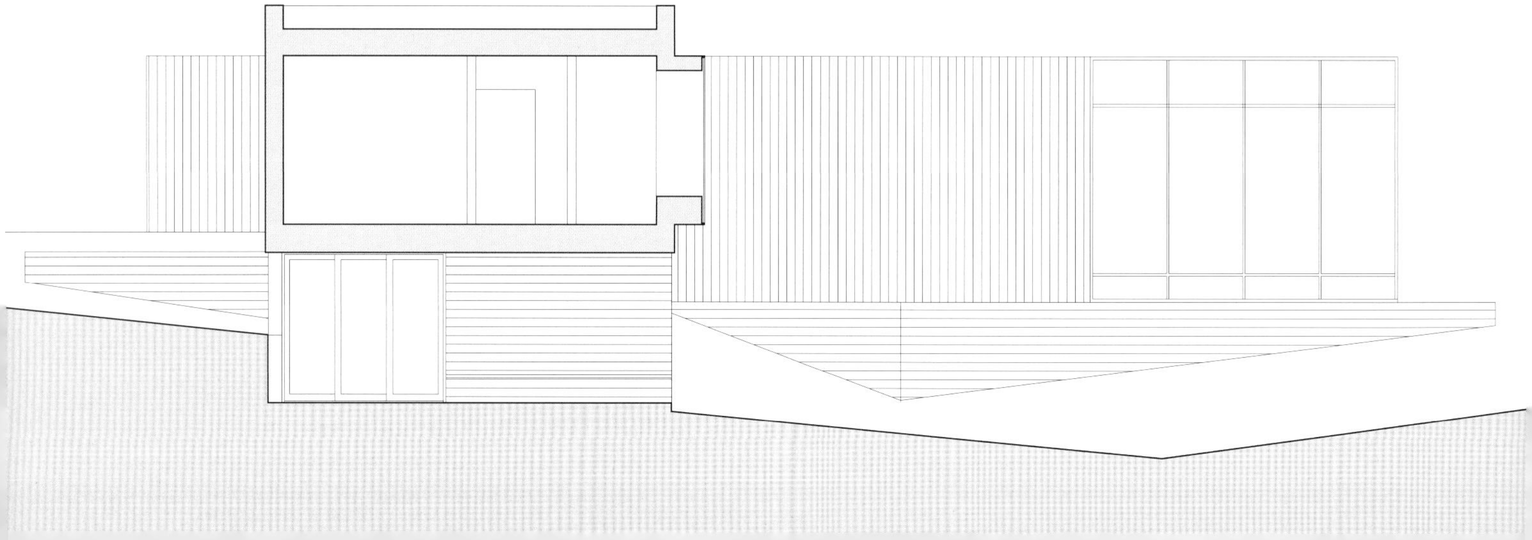

Image Captions		
	1	West facade (detail); © Matt Winquist
	2	Joinery studies
	3	Heuristic device (details)
	4	Exterior view; © Matt Winquist
	5	Site plan
		Building section
	6	North facade; © Matt Winquist
	7	Patio (detail); © Matt Winquist
	8	Exterior (detail); © Matt Winquist
	9	Final model, top view
	10	View of entrance; © Matt Winquist
		East facade; © Matt Winquist
	11	Entrance (detail); © Matt Winquist
	12	Southwest view; © Matt Winquist

Completed	2018
Size	4,950 SF (460 m^2)
Location	Salt Lake City, Utah
Team	John Sparano
	Anne Mooney
	Nate King
	Seth Striefel
	Drew Olguin (model)
Collaborators	McNeil Engineering (civil engineering)
	Structural Design Studio (structural engineering)
General Contractor	Living Home Construction

Firm Biography

Recognized as one of the top architecture firms in the world working in mountain settings, Sparano + Mooney Architecture is a practice based in the American West and engaged in a wide range of architectural explorations carefully crafted at multiple scales. The process-driven work has earned over fifty design awards and has been featured in publications and exhibitions around the world. This is the first monograph of the firm's work.

Biography of John Sparano

1961 Born in Bridgeport, Connecticut
1983 Bachelor of Architecture, the Catholic University of America, Washington, DC
1988 AA Diploma, Architectural Association School of Architecture, London, England
1990 Relocated to Los Angeles, California
1997 Established private practice with Anne Mooney in Los Angeles
2013 American Institute of Architects, Utah Chapter: Bronze Medal
2015 Elevated to the American Institute of Architects College of Fellows
2019 American Institute of Architects Western Mountain Region: Silver Medal

Biography of Anne Mooney

1962 Born in Butte, Montana
1987 Bachelor of Arts, University of Utah, Salt Lake City
1994 Graduate School of Architecture, Planning, and Preservation, Columbia University, New York
1995 Southern California Institute of Architecture, Ticino, Switzerland
1996 Master of Architecture (with distinction), Southern California Institute of Architecture, Los Angeles, California
1994 Began internship in the office of Eric Owen Moss Architects
1997 Established private practice with John Sparano in Los Angeles
2004 Appointed Assistant Professor of Architecture, University of Utah
2011 Promoted to Associate Professor of Architecture (with tenure), University of Utah
2011 Sabbatical in Rome, Italy
2014 American Institute of Architects Western Mountain Region: Young Architect of the Year
2016 University of Utah College of Architecture and Planning: Professor of the Year
2018 Promoted to Professor of Architecture, University of Utah
2020 Beverly Willis Architecture Foundation: Built by Women Award
2021 American Institute of Architects Western Mountain Region: Silver Medal

Sparano + Mooney Architecture Team: 1997–2022

The work in our office has been accomplished due, in no small part, to the incredible talent we have consistently been honored to collaborate with since establishing our practice. Experts in design, technically gifted, and skilled in project development and delivery, our team is extraordinarily talented. We are deeply grateful for the opportunity to share our days and work lives with each of them as we explore the possibilities of architecture together. Our collaborators have included the following individuals, with those listed in bold currently on our team.

Maxwell Altman
Michael James Atkinson
Matt Bean
John Becker
Jorge Beltran
Rene Berndt
Morgan Birch
Shelley Brady
Harrison Windsor Bush
Angela Clinkscales
Marco Colaiacomo
Philip Dimick
Michael Dolan
Camille Erickson
Mitch Gardner
Rebecca Gardner
Kelly Garfield
Stephanie Hatton
Matthew Hintze
Mark James
Ludwing Juarez
Colby Kalian
Daniel Kidd
Nate King
David Kirk
Simon Kwon
Soonju Kwon
Laurie Anne Larson
Jun Li
Randy Lu
Tomohisa Miyauchi
Jarrett Moe
Anne Mooney
PJ Nakamura
Diane Nielsen
Drew Olguin
Jake Ostlind
John Patrick Rooney
Luis Salas
Gabi Siu
Alexandra Smith
John Sparano
Michael Stebbins
Otto Aurek Stefan
Seth Striefel
Alan Taylor
Caitlin Thissen
Garrett Thompson
Jonathan Ware
Nathan Webster
Pingting Wei
Braden Wothuis
Mooc Wu
Liz Yonashiro
Ethan Zagorec-Marks
Mahnaz Zahiry
Elahe Zarezade

Firm Chronology
1997–2022

1997
- John Sparano and Anne Mooney establish Sparano + Mooney Architecture in Los Angeles, CA
- Reggie Rodriguez Community Center, Montebello, CA

1998
- Adaptive reuse of LAX former air-traffic control tower, Los Angeles, CA
- Exhibition of furniture design, BGH Gallery/ Bergamot Station Arts Center and Lindhurst Gallery, Los Angeles, CA

1999
- Gilb Museum of Arcadia Heritage, Arcadia, CA
- Design Exhibition, Third Street Promenade Gallery, Santa Monica, CA, and Wedge Gallery at Woodbury University, Burbank, CA

2000
- Andrew Cuomo tours Reggie Rodriguez Community Center

2001
- Exhibition: *New Blood*, 3A Garage Architecture Gallery, San Francisco, CA

2002
- American Institute of Architects, Foothill Chapter, Design Honor Award: Gilb Museum of Arcadia Heritage
- "Gilb Museum of Arcadia Heritage," *LA Architect*
- "Feature: Gilb Museum of Arcadia Heritage, Los Angeles," *A+U*, Layers of Wooden Architecture
- "Arcadia/Kalifornien: Gilb Museum of Arcadia Heritage," *Bauwelt*
- "Lessons from History: A New Museum by Sparano + Mooney," *World Architecture*
- "Point of Tension, A Case Study: Reggie Rodriguez Community Center," *Arc CA*
- "Project Portfolio: Community Centers, Reggie Rodriguez Community Center," *Architectural Record*

2003
- Queens Museum of Art Competition, Queens, NY
- Los Angeles Business Council Award for Outstanding Civic Architecture

2004
- Sparano + Mooney Architecture opens second office in Salt Lake City, Utah
- "Vibrazioni eteree: Gilb Museum of Arcadia Heritage," *L'Arca*
- "Los Angeles, Reggie Rodriquez Community Center," *Bauwelt*

2005
- Fisher Residence, Malibu, CA
- Utah Arts Council, Design Arts Award: Gilb Museum of Arcadia Heritage
- "New Designs: Reggie Rodriguez Community Center," *LA Architect*
- Exhibition: *Sacred Spaces*, City-County Gallery, Salt Lake City, UT
- Exhibition: *Gilb Museum of Arcadia Heritage*, Rio Gallery, Salt Lake City, UT

2006
- Star Valley Ranch Residence, Star Valley, WY
- Lakeview Performing Arts Center, Santa Fe Springs, CA
- Women's Concept Home, Daybreak, UT
- Utah Arts Council, Design Arts Award: Lakeview Performing Arts Center
- Utah Arts Council, Design Arts Award: Fisher Residence
- *2000+ New Architecture in Los Angeles*, Monacelli Press
- Exhibition, Southern California Institute of Architecture, Los Angeles, CA
- Exhibition: *Fisher Residence*, Rio Gallery, Salt Lake City, UT
- Exhibition: *Lakeview Performing Arts Center*, Rio Gallery, Salt Lake City, UT

2007
- Lou Costello Park Aquatic Center, Los Angeles, CA
- American Institute of Architects, Western Mountain Region, Design Award: Gilb Museum of Arcadia Heritage
- American Institute of Architects, Utah Chapter, Design Honor Award: Gilb Museum of Arcadia Heritage
- Utah Arts Council, Design Arts Award: Star Valley Ranch Residence
- Utah Arts Council, Design Arts Award: Women's Concept Home
- "Forest Theatrics: Lakeview Performing Arts Center," *Hinge Magazine*
- "Into the Woods: Lakeview Performing Arts Center," *Surface Magazine*
- Lecture, Skin Art and Ideas Festival, Pasadena, CA
- Exhibition: *Star Valley Ranch*, Rio Gallery, Salt Lake City, UT
- Exhibition: *Women's Concept House*, Rio Gallery, Salt Lake City, UT

2008
- Kennecott Visitor Center, South Jordan, UT
- Saint Joseph the Worker Catholic Church, West Jordan, UT
- City of Los Angeles Civic Architecture Award
- NEXT LA Design Award, Los Angeles Cultural Affairs Commission: Lou Costello Park Aquatic Center

- American Institute of Architects, Utah Chapter, Design Award: Saint Joseph the Worker Catholic Church (unbuilt)
- Lecture, Mobius LA, American Institute of Architects Design Conference, Los Angeles, CA
- Exhibition, Architecture + Design Museum, Los Angeles, CA

2009
- Emigration Canyon Residence, Salt Lake City, UT
- Downey Dental, Downey, CA
- American Institute of Architects, Western Mountain Region, Design Award: Saint Joseph the Worker Catholic Church (unbuilt)
- American Institute of Architects, Utah Chapter, Design Award: Emigration Canyon Residence
- "Housing an Idea: Star Valley Ranch," *Hinge Magazine*
- "Ultra Green Modern Maryfield Home," *Materialicious*
- "Top 10 Green Homes 2009," *Mother Nature News*
- "Ultra Modern Maryfield Home," *Jetson Green*
- Lecture, American Institute of Architects National Convention, San Francisco, CA
- Lecture: "New Directions in Residential Design," Salt Lake City Public Library, UT
- Design Week Exhibition and Open Studio: *Conceptual Constructs*, Salt Lake City, UT

2010
- American Institute of Architects, Western Mountain Region, Design Award: Emigration Canyon Residence
- "Canyon Residence," *Hinge Magazine* (cover story)
- "The New Pioneers," *Dwell Magazine*
- "A New Steel Home as Rugged as the Land," *Los Angeles Times*
- "Canyon Residence," *Detail Magazine*
- *Masterpieces: Chalet Architecture + Design*, Braun Publishing
- Lecture, Dwell on Design, Los Angeles, CA
- Moderator, Mountain West Arts Conference, Salt Lake City, UT

2011
- Saint Marguerite Elementary School, Tooele, UT
- Kimball Art Center Competition, Park City, UT
- Michel Gondry Film Club Exhibition, Museum of Contemporary Art, Los Angeles, CA
- Loop Bench, Manhattan Beach, CA
- "Saint Joseph the Worker," *Engineering News Record*
- "Sparano + Mooney: St. Joseph the Worker Catholic Church," *Grassroots Modern*
- *Small Eco Houses: Living Green in Style*, Rizzoli
- Lecture: Finalists for the Kimball Art Center Design Competition, Park City, UT

2012
- Notre Dame de L'Assomption Cathedral Competition, Port-au-Prince, Haiti
- Italian Hall Cultural Center, Los Angeles, CA
- American Institute of Architects, Utah Chapter, Architectural Firm of the Year Award
- American Institute of Architects, Western Mountain Region, Design Award: Saint Joseph the Worker Catholic Church
- Utah Arts Council, Design Arts Award: Strand Bench Designs
- Jury Prize, Utah Arts Council, Ten Years of Design Arts: Kimball Art Center
- American Concrete Institute, Excellence in Concrete Award: Saint Joseph the Worker Catholic Church
- "Sparano + Mooney's Kimball Art Center Proposal Takes Inspiration from Aspens," *Inhabitat*
- Lecture, American Institute of Architects, Oregon Design Conference, Portland, OR
- Lecture, Utah State University, Logan, UT
- Exhibition: *Kimball Art Center*, University of Utah, Salt Lake City, UT
- Exhibition: *Kimball Art Center*, Sundance Film Festival, Park City, UT

2013
- Fort Moore Pioneer Memorial, Los Angeles, CA
- Topaz Museum and Education Center, Delta, UT
- Bata del Norte New City Master Plan, Africa
- American Institute of Architects, Utah Chapter, Bronze Medal: John Sparano
- Utah Arts Council, Design Arts Award: Saint Joseph the Worker Catholic Church
- "Comfort Zone: A Magnetic House," *Sierra Magazine*
- "Sparano + Mooney: Church," *Domus Magazine*
- "Saint Joseph the Worker Catholic Church: Utah Church References Mining History," *Mark Magazine*
- "Divine Design," *Design Bureau*
- "Saint Joseph the Worker Catholic Church," *Architype Review: Religious Buildings*
- *Architectural Design for Contemporary Community Centers: Ideal Space Series*, Ifengspace Media
- "Gilb Museum of Arcadia Heritage," *Atlas of Contemporary World Architecture*, Phaidon
- "Canyon House," *Atlas of Contemporary World Architecture*, Phaidon
- "Saint Joseph the Worker Catholic Church," *Atlas of Contemporary World Architecture*, Phaidon
- Lecture, CoLab Gallery Speaker Series, Las Vegas, NV
- Exhibition: *Saint Joseph the Worker Catholic Church*, Rio Gallery, Salt Lake City, UT
- Exhibition: *World's Top 10 Mountain Architects, Dwell Magazine*, Powder Mountain, UT

2014
- Summit Powder Mountain Ski Lodge, Eden, UT
- Stuart Residence, Denver, CO
- Sipopo Performing Arts Center, West Africa
- Glashausen, Emigration Canyon, UT
- American Institute of Architects, Western Mountain Region, Young Architect of the Year: Anne Mooney
- Utah Arts Council, Design Arts Award: Topaz Museum and Education Center

- "Amazing Grace: Saint Joseph the Worker Catholic Church," *Utah Style & Design*
- "30 Most Beautiful Community Centers in the World: Reggie Rodriguez Community Center," *Social Work Centers*
- Lecture, American Institute of Architects, Central Utah Annual Conference, UT
- Lecture, American West Mayor's Symposium, Leonardo Museum, UT
- Strut Exhibit, University of Utah Marriott Library, Salt Lake City, UT
- Exhibition: *Best of Design Arts Utah: Kimball Art Center*, Traveling Exhibition, UT
- Exhibition: *Saint Joseph the Worker Catholic Church*, Utah Center for Architecture and AIA Architecture Week, UT
- Exhibition: *Emigration Canyon House*, Leonardo Museum, Salt Lake City, UT

2015
- Exhibition: *Matthew Barney: RIVER OF FUNDAMENT*, Museum of Contemporary Art, Los Angeles, CA
- Glenwild Residence, Park City, UT
- Pulsar Project, Salt Lake City, UT
- Thayne's Canyon Residence, Park City, UT
- American Institute of Architects, Faith and Form Religious Architecture Award: Saint Joseph the Worker Catholic Church
- John Sparano elected to the American Institute of Architects College of Fellows
- Utah Arts Council, Design Arts Award: Glashausen
- "Religious Architecture New Facilities: Saint Joseph the Worker Catholic Church," *Faith + Form*
- Lecture, Immersion Symposium, Goldwell, NV
- Lecture, American Institute of Architects, Colorado Design Conference, Keystone, CO
- Panelist, American Institute of Architects, Utah Fall Conference, Provo, UT
- Exhibition: *Glashausen*, Rio Gallery, Salt Lake City, UT

2016
- Pawley Aquatic Center, Indio, CA
- Utah State University Fine Arts Complex, Logan, UT
- Exhibition: *Doug Aitken*, Museum of Contemporary Art, Los Angeles, CA
- Central 9th Mixed-Use Development, Salt Lake City, UT
- Modern Farmhouse, Holladay, UT
- American Institute of Architects, Western Mountain Region, Architectural Firm of the Year Award
- Utah Arts Council, Design Arts Award: Pulsar Project
- American Planning Association, Utah Chapter Award: Taylorsville Master Plan
- Anne Mooney named Professor of the Year, University of Utah College of Architecture and Planning
- "A Home with a Sunny Outlook," *Wall Street Journal*
- "Sparano + Mooney Gets Top Architectural Award," *Salt Lake Tribune*
- "Modern Mountain House in a Utah Canyon," *Houzz*
- "Five of the Best Houses in Utah," *Dezeen*
- "Sparano + Mooney Clads Utah Residence in Hundreds of Scale-Like Steel Shingles," *Dezeen*
- "Opening Act," *Utah Style & Design*
- Lecture and Architectural Workshop, American Institute of Architects, Santa Fe, NM
- Lecture, Detroit-Volterra Foundation, Tuscany, Italy
- Lecture, University of Utah School of Architecture, Salt Lake City, UT
- Exhibition: *Pulsar Project*, Rio Gallery, Salt Lake City, UT

2017
- Studio City Net Zero Recreation Center, Los Angeles, CA
- Nora Eccles Harrison Museum of Art, Logan, UT
- Park City Community Center, Park City, UT
- Exhibition: *Don't Look Back: The 1990s at MOCA*, Museum of Contemporary Art, Los Angeles, CA
- Exhibition: *Adrián Villar Rojas: The Theater of Disappearance*, Museum of Contemporary Art, Los Angeles, CA
- American Society of Landscape Architects Award: Mountain Recreation Facilities Master Plan Project (with Landmark Design)
- American Planning Association, Utah Chapter Award: Town of Alta Commercial Core Plan (with Landmark Design)
- American Planning Association, Utah Chapter Award: Salt Lake Cultural Core (with the Cultural Planning Group and BWP Communications)
- Utah Arts Council, Design Arts Award: LOOP Bench Project
- "Park City Modern Residence by Sparano + Mooney Architecture," *Wall Street Journal*
- "After Four Decades, the Drought is about to End for Downtown L.A.'s Ft. Moore Hill Monument," *Los Angeles Times*
- "Top Architecture Firms in the West," *Mountain Living*
- "Renovation: USU Hall Reopens at 50th Anniversary Gala," *Utah Construction + Design*
- "Utah State University Gives an Extreme Makeover to its Main Concert Hall," *Salt Lake Tribune*
- "Heart of the Arts: USU to Unveil Renovated Chase Fine Arts Center," *Herald Journal*
- "Topaz Museum: Remembrance and Tribute, 75 Years On," *SL Underground Magazine*
- Exhibition: *Craft...Landscape...Place*, University of Nevada, Las Vegas, NV
- Exhibition: *LOOP Bench Project*, Rio Gallery, Salt Lake City, UT

2018
- Ludwing Juarez and Seth Striefel promoted to Principals
- Utah State University Multidisciplinary Design Center, Logan, UT
- Vipassana Buddhist Center, Banning, CA
- Bastian Agricultural Center, Herriman, UT
- Big Cartel Headquarters, Salt Lake City, UT
- *Zoe Leonard: Survey* and *Laura Owens* exhibitions, Museum of Contemporary Art, Los Angeles, CA
- American Institute of Architects, Utah Chapter, Design Honor Award: Nora Eccles Harrison Museum of Art

- "Powder Mountain Is the Hottest Design Destination You Probably Haven't Heard Of," *Architectural Digest*
- "A House Inspired by Petrified Wood," *Australian Design Review*
- "Gold Standard," *Mountain Living*
- "Bohemian Rhapsody," *Utah Style & Design*
- "A Historic Farmhouse Is Transformed into a Modern Home with a Green Roof," *Inhabitat*
- "Corten Steel Architecture: From the Atacama Desert to the Hills of California," *Wallpaper**
- "An Energy-Efficient Modern Church References Utah's Mining History," *Inhabitat*
- "Park City Modern House / Sparano + Mooney Architecture," *ArchDaily*
- "LEED Gold Home Celebrates Utah's Brilliant Light and Beauty," *Inhabitat*
- "Under the Radar: Reggie Rodriguez Community Center," *AIA California Council*
- Lecture, University of Utah and Detroit-Volterra Foundation, Tuscany, Italy

2019
- Aurora Villa Hotel, Fairbanks, AK
- Sundance Institute, Park City, UT (in collaboration with Elemental, Chile)
- Whittier Aquatic Center, Whittier, CA
- Equine Activity and Therapy Center, Logan, UT
- Exhibition: *40 for LA*, Museum of Contemporary Art, Los Angeles, CA
- Geffen Contemporary Building 5 Entry and Lobby, Museum of Contemporary Art, Los Angeles, CA
- Urban Treehouse, Salt Lake City, UT
- Wabi-Sabi Residence, Salt Lake City, UT
- American Institute of Architects, Western Mountain Region, Silver Medal: John Sparano
- American Institute of Architects, Utah Chapter, Design Award: Urban Treehouse
- *Architect's Newspaper* Design Award: Nora Eccles Harrison Museum of Art
- Utah Arts Council, Design Arts Award: Urban Treehouse
- Utah Arts Council, Design Arts Award: Nora Eccles Harrison Museum of Art
- *Off the Grid: Houses for Escape*, Thames & Hudson
- "Wyoming Canyon Residence by Sparano + Mooney Architecture," *Rethinking the Future*
- "Arcadia Museum," *Archello*
- "Sparano + Mooney Creates Sculptural Catholic Chapel for Utah Mining Town," *Dezeen*
- "Reggie Rodriguez Community Center," *Archello*
- Moderator, Architecture, Culture, and Spirituality Forum Symposium, Taliesin West, AZ
- Exhibition and Open Studio, Design Week, Salt Lake, UT
- Exhibition: *Nora Eccles Harrison Museum of Art*, Rio Gallery, Salt Lake City, UT
- Exhibition: *Urban Treehouse*, Rio Gallery, Salt Lake City, UT

2020
- Mother's Beach Boating Center, Los Angeles, CA
- Red Dirt Theater, Salt Lake City, UT
- Oikos Residence, Salt Lake City, UT
- Bonneville Residence, Salt Lake City, UT
- Lyric Theater, Logan, UT
- Gifted Music School, Salt Lake City, UT
- Powder Mountain Residence, Eden, UT
- American Institute of Architects, Utah Chapter, Design Award: Modern Farmhouse
- American Institute of Architects, Western Mountain Region, Design Honor Award: Urban Treehouse
- Beverly Willis Architecture Foundation, Built By Women Los Angeles 2020
- *Mountain Living*, Top Women in Architecture: Anne Mooney
- The Plan Award, International Culture Finalist: Nora Eccles Harrison Museum of Art
- The Plan Award, International House Finalist: Urban Treehouse
- "In Salt Lake City: A Modernist Man Cave," *New York Times*
- "Saint Joseph the Worker Day Chapel," *Architect's Newspaper*
- "Wooden Interiors and Copper Cladding Create Intimate Worship Space outside Salt Lake City," *Architect's Newspaper*
- "Utah Architecture: List of the Best Utah Buildings," *Salt Lake Tribune*
- "This Utah Home Coexists Naturally with the Environment," *Aspire*
- "Architects Share Best Practices for Working from Home," *Architectural Record*
- "Jaw-Dropping Homes in the Mountain West," *Dwell Magazine*
- "Standing Out and Fitting In: Renovation and Expansion of the Nora Eccles Harrison Museum of Art," *The Plan*
- "Sparano + Mooney Craft New Worship Center in Salt Lake City," *Contract Design*

2021
- American Institute of Architects, Utah Chapter, Honor Award: Wabi-Sabi
- Exhibition: *Pipilotti Rist: Big Heartedness, Be My Neighbor*, Museum of Contemporary Art, Los Angeles, CA
- Victory Ranch Residence, Kamas, UT
- Founders Place, Deer Valley, UT
- Colony at White Pine Canyon Residence, Park City, UT
- Sun Valley Residence, Sun Valley, ID
- Lo-Rise Housing Competition, Los Angeles, CA
- Prism House, Emigration Canyon, UT
- Interlaken, Midway, UT
- Homekey Transitional Housing, Los Angeles, CA
- *Residential Design*, 2021 National RD Award: Urban Treehouse
- "True to Utah: A Contemporary Interpretation of the Iconic American Farmhouse," *Mountain Living*
- Nate King promoted to Principal

2022
- Celebration of twenty-five years in practice as Sparano + Mooney Architecture

Acknowledgments

With gratitude, we acknowledge our team at Sparano + Mooney Architecture, with whom we have the honor and pleasure of creating architecture together. We are indebted to our partners Ludwing Juarez and Seth Striefel for our decades of collaboration and their skill and craft in designing and executing the work of the practice, and to Nate King, who led our team in producing the graphics for the book and always provides an insightful, thoughtfully constructive approach in developing the design work of our practice. We are grateful for the keen eye and steadfast guidance and support of our Studio Manager, Stephanie Hatton. Thank you also to our early mentor Norberto Martinez, who helped us get our start as we risked opening our office in Los Angeles, and to our friends and family for their ongoing support.

Thank you to Anne's colleagues at the University of Utah School of Architecture who have supported her academic and professional inquiry over the last fifteen years, and especially to the students who have continually inspired Anne to explore the boundaries of architecture and seek unconventional paths in pursuit of design. Special thanks to Thomas Carter for collaborative teaching and a shared research interest in the American West and to Martha Bradley Evans, who reviewed the first draft of the text.

This book is the result of collaborations with designer Michael Aberman and the publishing team at Hatje Cantz, Nicola von Velsen, Dorothee Hahn, and Stefanie Kruszyk, who provided thoughtful and creative guidance throughout the process.

Michael Webb (editor) is a Los Angeles-based writer who has authored more than twenty books on architecture and design—most recently, *Architects' Houses*; *Venice, CA: Art and Architecture in a Maverick Community*; *Architecture + Design LA*; and *Building Community: New Apartment Architecture*—while contributing essays to numerous publications. Webb is a regular contributor to leading journals in the United States and Europe. He is originally from London, where he was an editor at the *Times* and for *Country Life*, prior to relocating to the United States. Webb was awarded an honorary membership in the American Institute of Architects and made a Chevalier de l'Ordre des Arts et des Lettres for his services to French culture.

Hikmet Sidney Loe teaches art history at the University of Nevada, Las Vegas, and Westminster College in Salt Lake City, Utah. Her research on Robert Smithson's 1970 earthwork, *Spiral Jetty*, has led to the cumulative work *The Spiral Jetty Encyclo: Exploring Robert Smithson's Earthwork through Time and Place*. Exhibition catalogue essays were commissioned from Loe for *Utah Biennial: Mondo Utah* (Utah Museum of Contemporary Art, Salt Lake City) and *Plurality: Frank McEntire in Retrospect* (Snow College University, Utah). She has curated exhibitions at Westminster College, Finch Lane Gallery (Art Barn), Salt Lake City, and the Museum of Modern Art Library, New York. Loe also lectures frequently and exhibits photographs related to the land.

Colophon

Published by
Hatje Cantz Verlag GmbH
Mommsenstraße 27
10629 Berlin
www.hatjecantz.com

A Ganske Publishing Group Company

ISBN 978-3-7757-5058-5

Editor
Michael Webb

Project management
Dorothee Hahn

Copyediting
Sarah Stephenson

Proofreading
Benjamin Barlow

Graphic design
Michael Aberman
Kent Miller

Graphic design assistance
Sarah Hogg
Stockton Bermingham

Production
Stefanie Kruszyk, Hatje Cantz

Reproductions
Repromayer GmbH, Reutlingen

Printing and binding
Graspo

Cover illustration
Michael Aberman/Kent Miller (design) and
Sparano + Mooney Architecture (images)